CESS VOCABULARY

MAIN COURSE
Language and Skills
for Restaurant Workers

Renee Talalla

Falcon Press
MALAYSIA

FALCON PRESS SDN BHD (157710-H)
57A, Jalan 5/58, Gasing Indah
46000 Petaling Jaya, Selangor,
Malaysia

Tel: +603 77812303 / 77812308
Fax: +603 77812312
Email: falconp@po.jaring.my
Website: www.falconpub.com

First published 2000
© Asia-Pacific Press Holdings Ltd 2000

9 8 7 6 5 4
09 08 07 06 05 04

ISBN 983 9672 67 3 (Student Book)
ISBN 983 9672 68 1 (Student Book and Audio CD)

ACKNOWLEDGEMENTS
The author and publisher would like to thank the following for their advice
and assistance in the preparation of this book:

Sunda Kulendra, General Manager, Food and Beverage Catering Management,
Kuala Lumpur International Airport.

Philip Spencer, Renaissance Hotel, Kuala Lumpur.

Mohamed Sabarudin Talib, Restaurant Manager, Armada Hotel, Kuala Lumpur.

Cover design: Murad Hashim Associates Sdn Bhd

Printed in Malaysia by Prin-Ad Sdn. Bhd.

CONTENTS

NOTES TO THE USER

To the Student

If you are using this book on your own:
- Read through a Unit quickly. Use the pictures to help you guess the meanings of words you do not know.
- After the first reading, study the **Key Vocabulary** list with the help of the **Glossary** at the back of the book. Check the explanations of certain words and phrases in the **For Special Attention** box.
- Now go through the Unit again to make sure you understand all the vocabulary. Cover the captions under the pictures and try to describe the pictures using the vocabulary you have just learned.
- Try to memorize the **order** in which each task is done.
- Memorize the **expressions** given for each task. It is important to know the correct pronunciation and intonation of these expressions. Listen to the accompanying recording, or ask English speaking friends and colleagues to help you with this.
- Finally, do the **Exercises** in the Unit without referring to the previous pages. Check your answers in the **Answer Key** at the back of the book.
- Role-play the **dialogues** in the Exercise pages with an English-speaking friend if possible.

Note: Although you probably normally use a bilingual dictionary for words you do not understand, try to use the glossary at the back of the book, as a first step towards using an English only dictionary.

To the Teacher / Trainer

This book can be used as the basic resource material for a training course for restaurant service attendants, or as a supplement to existing training material. The main **advantages** of this book are that:
- the basic **vocabulary** needed by the trainee is given in the book, and also listed in the Glossary.
- lexical items are better **understood** by trainees with only a basic level of proficiency in English, because job-specific words and actions are clearly and graphically depicted in the picture frames.
- the Picture Process layout of each task should enable the trainee to better **remember** the order in which each task is performed.
- the **role plays** contained in the exercise pages of the units **reinforce** the use of common **expressions** that recur constantly in restaurant work.

SUGGESTED USE OF THE BOOK
Trainers / teachers have the option of using the book in one or all of the ways listed below:
- as a **course book** or main text for a training course for restaurants service attendants
- to **equip** trainees with **job-specific vocabulary** before or during a training session.
- to **reinforce** training sessions with the written exercises and role-plays from each Unit.
- as a take-home **reminder** of a training session.
- as a preliminary **introduction** before the training session for any aspect of restaurant work.

AUTHOR'S NOTE
The material in this book cannot cover every aspect of restaurant work or all the variables of interaction or communication that arise in actual situations in restaurants. Trainers may need to expand on the material in each Unit to cover additional tasks and situations. With knowledge and acquisition of basic vocabulary, trainees should be able to role-play further situations that commonly occur in the course of their job.

Language trainers may need to deal with any structural difficulties that arise as this is outside the scope of this book.

Trainers need to pay particular attention to the trainees' *pronunciation* and *intonation* when using the functional expressions in the book. Use of the accompanying recording, and tape recording the trainees themselves during role-plays, would help them hear and improve their spoken language.

As far as possible, the material in the book follows the standard practice of service in international western-food restaurants. Trainers may need to make changes and adjustments to reflect the practice of the establishments they serve.

ABOUT THIS BOOK

Objectives

To provide front line personnel in restaurants with:
- The job-related *vocabulary and language* needed for work in this field.
- The basic *skills* needed to perform the various tasks in restaurant work.

The User

The book is designed for use by:
- The *trainee waiter or waitress* [high elementary level English upwards], who needs the specific vocabulary and commonly used expressions for their job.
- Any English speaking, *entry-level restaurant employee* who needs an easy-to-follow guide to the various tasks in restaurant work.
- The restaurant *trainer or language instructor,* whose job can be supplemented and facilitated by the material in this book.

The Material

The material in this book reflects as far as possible the standard practice of international western food restaurants. Users may need to make some minor adjustments to fit the practice and regulations of the establishments they serve.
- The main **tasks** in restaurant work are treated in fifteen separate units. Each unit shows a clear step-by-step depiction of a particular task in a **picture process** format. Captions below each picture frame contain the vocabulary needed for that task.
- Speech balloons in the picture frames give basic functional **expressions** for that particular task.
- **Key Vocabulary** boxes at the end of each Unit list all the important and useful words for the given task.
- **For Special Attention** boxes in each Unit explain idioms and certain words and phrases more fully.
- **Five-pointed stars** throughout the book give additional occupational tips.
- Other common functional expressions for each task are given in the **More Expressions** boxes.
- The **Glossary** at the back of the book is a list of basic food and service related lexical items. It can serve as a useful guide, for both students and trainers, to the target vocabulary needed at this level.
- A **recording** of the main text, the additional expressions and the dialogues from the exercises pages are available separately.

Organization

- Each unit is a four-page spread.
  - The first two facing pages depict a particular restaurant task in pictures with captions below. Key vocabulary and expressions for the task are given in boxes on these pages.
  - The following two facing pages consist of exercises, word puzzles, role-plays etc., which incorporate the target vocabulary and expressions covered in the unit.
- The volume also contains
  - an answer key to the exercises.
  - a glossary of basic job-related words and phrases.

RESTAURANT STAFF

The number and categories of staff in a restaurant will vary according to the size of the restaurant.

manager

assistant manager

head waiter or *maitre d'hotel* [abbr. *Maitre d'*]

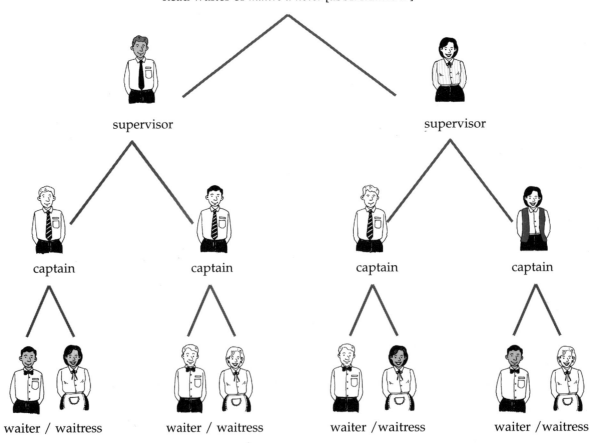

supervisor   supervisor

captain   captain   captain   captain

waiter / waitress   waiter / waitress   waiter /waitress   waiter /waitress

Back of House:

Stewards whose duties include taking away and washing up used dishes etc from the Service or Clearing Station.
Cleaners who clean, dust and vacuum the restaurant after each meal sitting.

PLAN OF A RESTAURANT

Restaurants may have some or all of the following features:

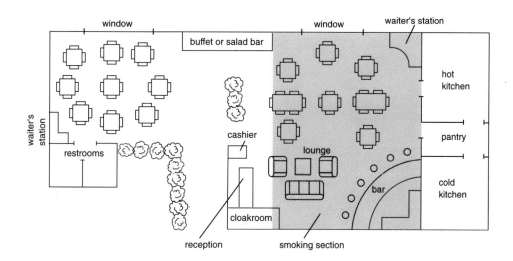

SOME PARTS OF A RESTAURANT

Bar

Kitchen (hot)

Pantry

Reception desk

Cloakroom

Cashier

THE EQUIPMENT: CUTLERY / GLASSWARE

CUTLERY [Silverware or Flatware]

KNIVES

table fish steak butter fruit carving cake slice

FORKS

table fish dessert fruit oyster cake carving service

SPOONS

table soup dessert tea / coffee demitasse ice-cream sauce service

GLASSWARE

water wine beer champagne

tumbler *goblet* *flute* *bowl*

liqueur sherry brandy longdrink or hiball glass cocktail

martini *tumbler*

THE EQUIPMENT: CROCKERY / OTHER

CROCKERY [China]

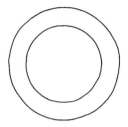
dinner plate

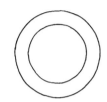
fish / salad plate

side /
bread plate

soup /
cereal bowl

butter dish

pepper and
salt shakers

tea / coffee cup
and saucer

demitasse
and saucer

teapot

coffeepot

milk jug
or creamer

sugar bowl

OTHER These items are commonly used in restaurants.

tray stand

wine-bucket stand

tray

service plate

bread basket

tablecloth

napkin or serviette

placemat

stirrer

coaster

7

COOKING METHODS

Restaurant customers often ask how a dish is prepared or cooked. Here are some of the main methods of cooking food.

Boiling

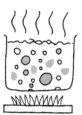

Food is cooked in deep boiling liquid [water, stock, wine etc.] in an open or covered saucepan.

Simmering

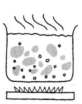

Like boiling, but the liquid is kept just below boiling point in an uncovered pot.

Steaming

Food is placed on a container and cooked in the steam from boiling water in a covered pan or steamer.

Stewing

Cooking food in its own juices with a little additional liquid, in a covered pan, at simmering point.

Braising

Pieces of food are first browned in a little fat, then cooked with some liquid in a closed pan.

Deep-frying

Frying pieces of food in a deep pot or fryer with plenty of hot oil or fat.

Sautéing

Cooking small or thin pieces of food in a little very hot oil or fat. The frying pan is shaken constantly to stop the food from burning.

Flambéing

After frying, alcohol is added to the food in the frying pan and set on fire. This gives added flavour to the food.

Pan-frying

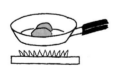

Frying food in a little oil or butter using a frying pan over moderate heat.

Broiling / grilling

Cooking food like steak or fish, over or under open heat, e.g. under the oven grill, or on a barbecue or hot plate.

Roasting

Cooking food like meat or poultry with some fat in a hot oven [between 200-240 degrees centigrade].

Baking

Cooking food like cakes, pies, bread etc. in a closed oven at a temperature of between 120-240°C.

FOOD: SEAFOOD / POULTRY

SEAFOOD

The term seafood covers all fish from the sea or freshwater as well as shellfish.

FISH
Names of some sea and freshwater fish.

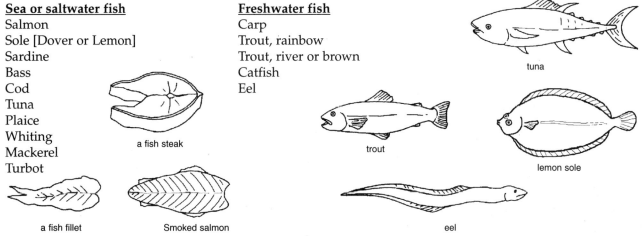

Sea or saltwater fish
Salmon
Sole [Dover or Lemon]
Sardine
Bass
Cod
Tuna
Plaice
Whiting
Mackerel
Turbot

Freshwater fish
Carp
Trout, rainbow
Trout, river or brown
Catfish
Eel

a fish steak

trout

tuna

lemon sole

a fish fillet

Smoked salmon

eel

SHELLFISH

The following shellfish are often served in restaurants.

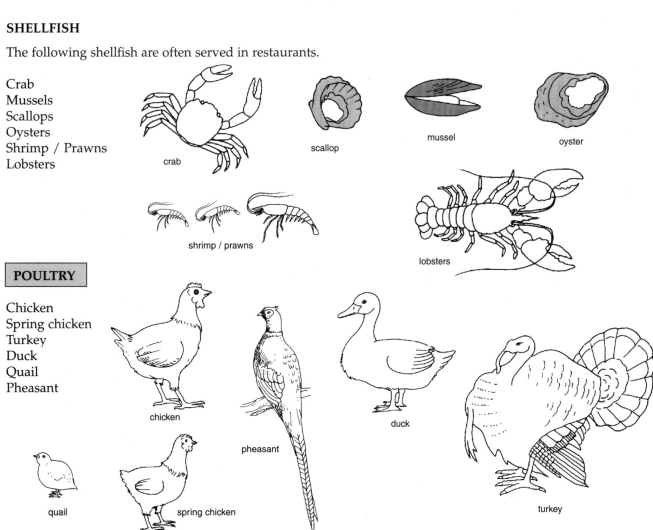

Crab
Mussels
Scallops
Oysters
Shrimp / Prawns
Lobsters

crab

scallop

mussel

oyster

shrimp / prawns

lobsters

POULTRY

Chicken
Spring chicken
Turkey
Duck
Quail
Pheasant

chicken

pheasant

duck

turkey

quail

spring chicken

FOOD: MEAT

Meat dishes served in restaurants are prepared from one of the following meats:

BEEF   LAMB   VEAL   PORK   VENISON

The diagrams below are simplified to show only the major commercial cuts.
Names of these cuts and joints vary from country to country.

BEEF

[1] Lean meat that needs long, slow cooking. Used for stews, casseroles and ground [minced] beef dishes e.g. hamburgers, meatloaf, meat sauce for pasta etc.

[2] Lean meat with good flavour. Used for grilling [rump steak], braising, or pot roasting.

[3 & 4] Steaks such as sirloin, porterhouse, entrecote, rib-eye and t-bone come from this section. Also used for dishes like kebabs, roast beef and beef ribs.

[5] Lean, boneless meat that is very tender and very expensive. Used for dishes like Chateaubriand, Fillet Mignon, Beef Tournedos, Beef Bourguignon, etc.

[6] The rib portion of this cut is used for roasting. Chuck or blade steak from this section is used for slow cooking casseroles or stews.

[7 & 8] Inexpensive and rather fatty meat. Used for corned beef, pot roasts or slow braising. Meat from the flank is also used for beef roulades or paupiettes [rolls], flank steak, pot roasts.

LAMB

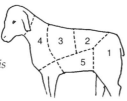

Lamb is the flesh of young animals of between 3–12 months old. The term 'muttom' is used for the flesh of older sheep.

[1] A large roasting joint often served in restaurants as Roast Leg of Lamb.

[2] Loin joints can be roasted whole or boned and rolled. The loin is also cut up into loin chops for grilling, frying or barbecuing.

[3] This section has the best chops or cutlets for grilling or frying etc. It is also used for the well-known dishes, Crown Roast and Rack of Lamb.

[4 & 5] The shoulder and breast meat can be used for kebabs, casseroles, and dishes that require stewing or braising. A boned and rolled shoulder makes a tasty and less expensive roast.

VEAL

Veal is the flesh of very young calves. It is an expensive meat that is pale in colour and very tender. As veal is rather dry and bland, it needs sauces, stuffings and seasonings to provide additional flavour. Many fine dining restaurants include veal dishes on their menus.

[1] Slices of meat from this section are called by several names, e.g. scallops, escalopes, scallopini, schnitzels or cutlets. These pieces of veal are prepared in many different ways.

[2] This section can be boned and rolled for roasts, or cut up into chops for grilling, frying, braising, etc. Crown roasts and veal cutlets are also from this section.

[3] The shoulder joint is also often boned, stuffed and rolled for roasts.

[4] Breast meat is often used for stewing or braising. It can also be rolled and stuffed for a roast.

[5 & 6] Shanks are used for stewing or braising. Osso Bucco is a popular Italian dish made from this cut.

PORK

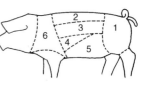

The most common cuts of pork used in restaurants are from the leg [1], loin [3], and rib [4] sections.

[1] Excellent for roast pork and ham – two of the best-known pork dishes.

[3] Meat from this section provides loin chops for grilling, baking or frying, as well as the popular Crown Roast. The pork fillet or tenderloin is also from this section.

[4] Spare ribs are a popular choice in restaurants. They can be baked, barbecued, grilled or braised.

[5] Flank or belly pork is used for stews or braised dishes, and especially for curing as bacon.

VENISON

Venison is the flesh of young male deer.
The roasted leg joint, steaks and braised loin or neck chops are some venison dishes served in restaurants.

FOOD: VEGETABLES

The vegetables listed below are among some of the commonly used vegetables in restaurants.
They are grouped under the following categories:
- Root vegetables
- Green vegetables
- Non-leafy vegetables
- Herbs and seasonings

GREEN VEGETABLES

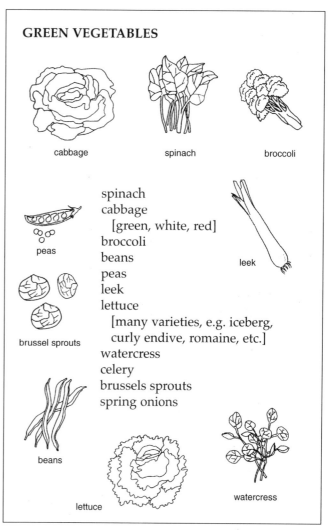

cabbage   spinach   broccoli

spinach
cabbage
  [green, white, red]
broccoli
beans
peas
leek
lettuce
  [many varieties, e.g. iceberg,
  curly endive, romaine, etc.]
watercress
celery
brussels sprouts
spring onions

peas

brussel sprouts

leek

beans

lettuce

watercress

ROOT VEGETABLES

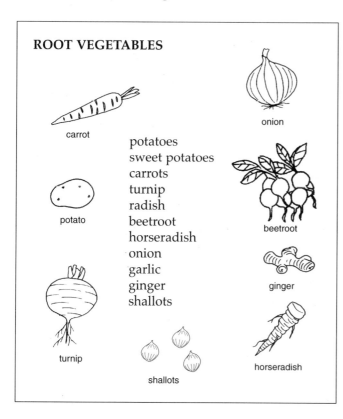

carrot

onion

potatoes
sweet potatoes
carrots
turnip
radish
beetroot
horseradish
onion
garlic
ginger
shallots

potato

beetroot

ginger

turnip

shallots

horseradish

NON-LEAFY VEGETABLES

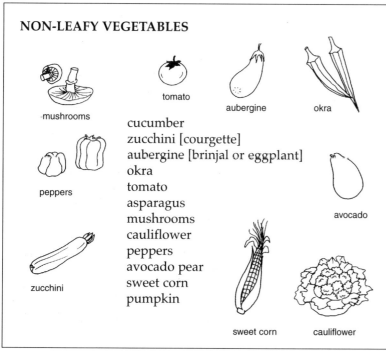

mushrooms

tomato

aubergine

okra

cucumber
zucchini [courgette]
aubergine [brinjal or eggplant]
okra
tomato
asparagus
mushrooms
cauliflower
peppers
avocado pear
sweet corn
pumpkin

peppers

avocado

zucchini

sweet corn   cauliflower

HERBS AND SEASONINGS

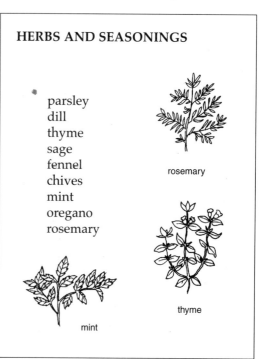

parsley
dill
thyme
sage
fennel
chives
mint
oregano
rosemary

rosemary

mint

thyme

BEVERAGES: NON-ALCOHOLIC

HOT DRINKS

COFFEE

Restaurants may serve a variety of coffees from various parts of the world, e.g. Brazil, Columbia, Kenya, Indonesia etc.

There are also many ways of serving coffee. The most well-known of these are:

Espresso – a strong black coffee served in a demitasse or small cup.

Cappuccino – milk which has been frothed up with steam is added to strong black coffee.

Latte – coffee made with hot milk and usually served in a large cup or tall glass 'mug'.

Regular coffee – black coffee to which milk or sugar can be added.

Decaffeinated coffee – coffee that does not contain caffeine, [a stimulant found in tea and coffee].

TEA

Tea is grown in many regions of the world, e.g. Sri Lanka, India, China. It is made by pouring boiling water over tea-leaves or teabags.

Tea is served with milk, sugar or a slice of lemon.

Herbal Teas – tea made by pouring boiling water over the leaves of plants such as Camomile, Mint or other herbs.

Herbal teas are usually served without milk.

HOT CHOCOLATE

Hot Chocolate – a drink made by mixing powdered chocolate with hot milk.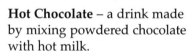

COLD DRINKS

FRUIT / VEGETABLE JUICES

Shown below are some fruit and vegetables that can be freshly squeezed to extract juice.

apple   carrot   guava   grapefruit   honeydew

mango   pineapple   watermelon   tomato   lemon/lime

BOTTLED / CANNED DRINKS

These drinks are sometimes referred to as *soft drinks*. In the USA any carbonated [i.e. with gas bubbles] drink is called a *soda*.

Listed below are some well-known soft drinks.

cola (e.g. **Pepsi, Coke**)
**ginger ale   ginger beer
tonic   soda water
bitter lemon   lemonade
mineral water**
[either *carbonated / aerated*, or *still*, i.e. without gas bubbles]

BEVERAGES: ALCOHOLIC

Alcoholic beverages commonly served in restaurants are grouped under the following categories:

Spirits	**Wines**	**Fortified wines**
Beer	**Cocktails**	**Liqueurs**

WINES

Alcohol made from the fermented juice of black or white grapes. [Wine can also be made from other fruits, but these wines are not drunk with meals.]
There are four types of wine made from grapes.

Red wine – made from black grapes. The colour is obtained from pigment in the grape skin during the fermentation period.

White wine – made from white and black grapes. The skins are removed before fermentation.

Rose – a pale pink wine made from white and black grapes. The skins are removed before fermentation is completed.

Sparkling wine – luxury wines that are filled with bubbles of gas by special production methods. The gas is kept in the bottle by wiring down the cork.
The most famous sparkling wine comes from the Champagne region in France.

SPIRITS

Spirits are strong, distilled, alcoholic drinks made from grain [e.g. barley, rye] or other plants. These drinks are often served with mixers such as tonic, soda, bitter lemon etc.

Bourbon
Brandy
Whisky
Gin
Rum
Vodka
Campari

FORTIFIED WINES

Wine that is strengthened by the addition of alcohol, usually brandy.
The most well-known fortified wines are:

Madeira	**Sherry**
Port	**Vermouth**
Marsala	

COCKTAILS

These drinks are made by mixing or shaking liquor and/ or wine with other ingredients. Cocktails are drunk before a meal.
Here are the names of some popular cocktails:

Black Russian
Black Velvet
Bloody Mary
Daiquiri
Gimlet
Gin Fizz
Manhattan
Margarita
Martini
Mimosa
Rum Punch
Singapore Sling
Tom Collins
Whisky sour

LIQUEURS

Liqueurs are strong, sweet spirits made from many different fruits, grain or plants.
They are served after a meal in a small glass.
Some well-known liqueurs are:

Amaretto
Bailey's Irish Cream
Benedictine
Chartreuse
Cherry Brandy
Cointreau
Crème de Cacao
Crème de Menthe
Curacao
Drambuie
Grand Marnier
Khalua
Tia Maria

BEER

An alcoholic drink brewed from malted barley, sugar and hops, then fermented with yeast.
The main types of beer are:

Ale – this has a strong hop flavour and is more bitter than lager beers.

Dark beer – made from malt toasted to a darker colour than normal.

Lager – this beer is light-bodied and light coloured.

Stout – similar to ale but heavier, darker and a little sweeter. Very dark malt is used in the brewing.

Taking Reservations by Telephone

1. Fred, the head waiter, answered the telephone at Chez Max. He greeted the caller...

Good afternoon.

2. ...and identified the restaurant and himself.

...Chez Max. Fred speaking.

3. He offered to assist the caller.

May I help you?

4. The caller wished to make a dinner reservation. Fred got out the reservation notepad.

I'd like to make a dinner reservation, please.

Certainly, madam.

5. He asked her for the date of the reservation...

For what date, please?

6. ...and wrote down the details as she spoke.

The fourteenth of February.

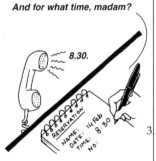

7. He found out the time of the reservation.

And for what time, madam?

8.30.

8. Fred asked the caller for her name. She spelt it out for him.

May I have your name, please?

Yes, it's Reid. Ms Reid. That's R-E-I-D.

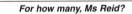

9. Fred asked Ms Reid for the number of people in her party.

For how many, Ms Reid?

For four.

10. The caller had a special request – a window table.

I'd like a table in non-smoking, by the window.

11. Fred checked the floor chart.

Just a minute, Ms Reid, I'll see if we have a table.

12. He apologized because the non-smoking section was booked out that night.

I'm very sorry, Ms Reid, but there are no tables left in non-smoking.

13. He offered her an alternative, and asked for her agreement.

We have a window table in smoking. Would you care for that?

14. Ms Reid accepted the offer.

Yes, all right.

15. Fred read back to Ms Reid all the details he had written on the reservation notepad.

So that's a window table for four, at eight-thirty, on the fourteenth of February.

★ Addressing Guests

Whenever possible use:
SIR / MADAM
or
MR / MRS / MS / TITLE + name
when you speak to guests.

Could I have a contact number, please?

Yes. It's 7745632.

16. He asked Ms Reid for a contact number and wrote it down on the notepad.

Thank you for calling...

17. Before ending the conversation, Fred thanked the caller...

...We'll see you on the fourteenth. Goodbye, Ms Reid.

18. ...and said goodbye.

⭐ Speaking about TIME:

At eight o'clock
At eight

At a quarter past eight
At eight fifteen

At eight thirty
At half past eight

At a quarter to eight
At seven forty-five

⭐ Speaking about DATES

Written: 1 Jan   1/1   1.1. 2001
Spoken: *January first*
       The first of January

Written: 31 Dec 31/12 12.31.2001
Spoken: *December thirty-first*
      The thirty-first of December

Written: 14 Feb 14/2   2.14.2001
Spoken: *February fourteenth*
      The fourteenth of February

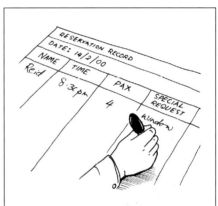

19. Finally Fred copied all the information on the notepad into the restaurant reservation record.

KEY VOCABULARY

VERBS
accept
address
answer
apologize
ask [for]
assist
care for
   [something]
check
copy
end
find [out]
get out
   [something]
greet
identify
make
   [a reservation]
offer
reserve
spell
take
   [a reservation]
write

NOUNS
agreement
alternative
caller
contact number
date
details
floor chart
head waiter
information
notepad
number
party
record
request
reservation
section
title
window
waiter

OTHERS
booked out
instead
non-smoking
smoking
special

FOR SPECIAL ATTENTION

- *make a reservation* = the caller makes a reservation.
- *take a reservation* = the waiter takes a reservation
- *A floor chart* is a plan showing all the tables and parts of the restaurant.
- *details* = small items of information
- *A reservation record* is a book that contains all the details of reservations.
- *a booking* = a reservation
- *booked out / fully booked* = the restaurant is full and can't take any more reservations
- *a special request* = the caller asks for something more, e.g. a window table, or a birthday cake etc.
- *identify yourself* = say who you are
- *a party* = a group
- *offered her an alternative* = gave her another choice or possibility

NB: Some women prefer to use the title *MS*, instead of *MRS* or *MISS*.

MORE EXPRESSIONS

Picture

3 *"How can I help you, sir?"*

5 *"For which day?"*

7 *"What time is the reservation for?"*
   "At what time?"

8 *"Could I have your name, please?"*
   "Under what name?"

9 *"For how many people?"*

11 *"I'll check if we have a table."*

16 *"Could you give me a contact number, please?"*

18 *"We look forward to seeing you on the fourteenth."*

15

UNIT 1 – Exercises

1. Choose a word from the box to match each picture below.

notepad	floor chart	caller	date	window table
reservation record	waiter	non-smoking sign		

_____   _____   _____   _____
    waiter

 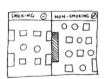 

_____   _____   _____   _____

2. Fred asked the caller for the details of the reservation. What information did Fred ask for?

date of reservation
_____   _____

_____   _____

_____   _____

_____

3. Match the words in column A with their meanings in column B.

	A		B
1.	assist.............................[e]	a.	give your name
2.	reserve.........................[ ]	b.	no more seats /tables
3.	a group.........................[ ]	c.	say sorry
4.	a request.....................[ ]	d.	say yes to an offer
5.	fully booked...............[ ]	e.	help
6.	apologize....................[ ]	f.	book
7.	accept..........................[ ]	g.	a party
8.	identify yourself..........[ ]	h.	something a person asks for

16

4. Write out some ways of _saying_ the time shown on the clocks below.

seven fifteen
or
a quarter past seven

_____ _____ _____ _____

_____ _____ _____ _____

5. Write down a _spoken_ form of these dates.

April 5   23 May   12th Dec   2.6.2000   31/12

the fifth of April   _____   _____   _____   _____

6. Match the terms on the left with the statements on the right.

1. Identifying yourself   [c]   a. "a round table near the door"

2. Greeting   [   ]   b. "I'm afraid we're fully booked tonight."

3. A special request   [   ]   c. "Jenny speaking."

4. Apologizing   [   ]   d. "Good afternoon, sir."

5. Spelling out something   [   ]   e. "Can I help you, madam?"

6. Making a reservation   [   ]   f. "I'll check the floor chart for you."

7. Assisting a caller   [   ]   g. "That's H-U-D-S-O-N."

8. Offering to do something   [   ]   h. "I'd like to book a table for dinner, please."
   for someone

7. What is the head waiter saying to the callers below? Fill in the speech bubbles

8. Discuss the following questions with your trainer or partner.

1. Why do some women prefer to use the title MS instead of MISS or MRS?

2. Why did Fred ask the caller for a contact number?

3. Why does Fred write down details on a notepad while he talks to the caller?

Receiving and Seating Guests

Good evening. Welcome to Chez Max. Do you have a reservation, sir?

Yes. The name's Nicols.

1. Fred greeted the people at the reception desk and asked if they had a reservation.

Ah yes, Mr Nicols, a table for four in smoking?

Yes, that's right.

2. He checked the Reservation Record and confirmed the details with the guest.

I'll show you to your table, sir. This way, please.

3. Fred showed Mr Nicols and his party to table 14, which was reserved for them.

Will this be all right, Mr Nicols?

Yes, this is fine, thank you.

4. He asked if they were satisfied with the table.

Allow me, madam.

5. Fred pulled out the chair of the lady guest closest to him...

6. ...and slowly pushed the chair back into position as the guest was seating herself.

Excuse me, madam.

7. Standing to the right of the guest, Fred picked up the napkin,...

8. ...folded it into a triangular shape...

Excuse me, madam.

9. ...and placed it on the guest's lap.

Your waiter will be with you shortly. I hope you have a good dinner.

10. He told the guests that a waiter would attend to them soon.

Leading Guests to the Table

- Walk about two paces ahead of the guests.

- Point in the direction of the table with palm open and arm extended.

11. He then returned to the reservation desk.

A table for two in smoking, please. We don't have a reservation.

12. The next guests to arrive did not have a reservation.

Yes, we have a table for you, madam.

13. He checked the floor chart and found a table for them.

Talking to guests

- Speak clearly. Smile and make eye contact.

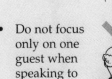

- Do not focus only on one guest when speaking to a group.

Can I take your coats? *Oh yes, thank you.*

14. Fred offered to keep their coats in the cloakroom.

Would you mind waiting a few minutes? We'll get the table ready for you now.

15. He asked them to wait while the table was being prepared.

KEY VOCABULARY

VERBS
allow
arrive
attend
check
focus
fold
get (something ready)
greet
make [eye contact with]
pick [up]
place
point
prepare
pull [out]
push [in]
receive
return
seat
show
smile
wait
welcome

NOUNS
arm
chair
cloakroom
coat
desk
details
direction
eye-contact
floor chart
lap
napkin
palm
party
position
shape

OTHERS
ahead
clearly
closest
extended
reserved
satisfied
shortly

FOR SPECIAL ATTENTION

- *details* = small items of information
- *seating herself* = the action of sitting down
- *two paces* = two steps [about 1 metre]
- *ahead* = in front of
- *satisfied with* = pleased with
- *a table for four* = a table which can seat four people
  a table of four = there are four people at the table
- *cloakroom* = a place where coats, hats, umbrellas, parcels etc. can be left for a time.
- *stand to the right of someone* = stand on the right hand side of that person
- *make eye contact with someone* = to look directly into the eyes of someone
- *focus only on one guest* = look only at one person
- *triangular* = in the shape △ of a triangle

NB: The smoking and non-smoking sections of a restaurant are usually referred to as 'smoking' or 'non-smoking'.

MORE EXPRESSIONS

Picture

1 "Have you got a reservation, sir?"

3 "Let me show you to your table."
"Could you follow me, please?"

5 "Let me help you, madam."

13 "Yes. There is a table available"

14 "Would you like to leave your coats here?"

15 "I hope you don't mind waiting a few minutes."
"Could you please wait a few minutes?"

UNIT 2 – Exercises

1. What is the waiter doing in the pictures below?
Choose an action word from the box to fill in the blanks.

| pulling out | picking up | showing |
| seating | folding | welcoming |

1. He is _____ them to the table.

2. He is _____ the chair.

3. He is _____ the guest.

4. He is _____ the plate.

5. He is _____ the napkin.

6. He is _____ the guests.

2. Solve the word puzzle with the help of the clues below. Choose from the words on the right. Be careful! You only need eight of the fifteen words.

1. You sit on this.
2. A shape with three sides.
3. A distance of about half a metre, or one step.
4. Small items of information.
5. The inside surface of your hand.
6. A group of people.
7. A piece of cloth or paper used while eating.
8. A mother often holds her baby on this while sitting.

party
direction
number
fingers
time
lap
napkin
table
chair
pace
palm
triangle
date
leg
details

3. Choose words from the Key Vocabulary list that can replace the underlined words in the sentences.

1. He missed the bus because there were too many people *in front* of him.   [_Eg. ahead_]

2. The customers were very *pleased* with the good service in that restaurant.   [_____]

3. He is easy to understand because he speaks *slowly and carefully*.   [_____]

4. The waiter took their drinks order *a few minutes* after they sat down.   [_____]

5. He smiled and *looked directly at* the pretty girl in the room.   [_____]

6. The old lady asked the man, *who was next* to her, to help her with her bag.   [_____]

20

4. What is the waiter saying to the guests in the pictures below?
Put the correct picture number next to the waiter's statements.

a. "Could you follow me, please."

b. "Your waiter will be with you shortly."

c. "Allow me."

d. "Is this all right for you?"

5. Complete the dialogue below between the waiter and the guests.

[*Two ladies enter the restaurant. They come to the reception desk.*]

Waiter: [*Greet and welcome the guests*] ....

Guest: Good evening. A table for two, please.

Waiter: [*Ask if they have a reservation*] ....

Guest: No, we don't.

Waiter: [*Find out where they would like to sit.*] ....

Guest: Non-smoking, please.

Waiter: [*Tell them that a table is available. Ask them politely to wait a few minutes.*] ....

....

Guest: Yes, that's fine. We'll wait over there.

Waiter: [*Ask about their coats.*] ....

Guest: Oh, yes. Thank you.

Waiter: [*10 minutes later: Tell them the table is ready and you will take them to it.*] ....

....

6. Role-play the above dialogue with your partner. Don't forget to exchange roles.

7. Discuss the questions below with your trainer or partner.

1. Why is it important to make eye contact when you speak to someone?

2. Why do most restaurants have separate smoking and non-smoking areas?

Taking a Beverage Order

Good evening. My name's Mary. I'll be serving your table this evening.

1. Mary, the waitress for table 14, introduced herself.

Here's our menu, sir.

2. She gave each guest the à la carte menu.

Would you like to order a drink before dinner?

3. She asked if the guests wanted an aperitif.

A dry sherry, please.

Certainly, madam. And for you, madam?

4. She took their orders in a clockwise direction,...

5. ...and wrote the details down on the beverage order form.

That's one gin and tonic, one dry sherry, and two beers.

Yes, that's right.

6. Mary repeated the whole order to make sure it was correct.

Order for table 14.

7. She gave one copy of the order to the bartender.

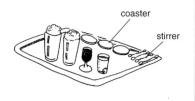

coaster

stirrer

8. When the drinks were ready, Mary arranged them on a tray. She also put some coasters and stirrers on the tray.

9. She took the drinks to the table, and served the lady on the right of the host first.

Your gin and tonic, madam.

10. Mary placed the lady's drink on a coaster, near the wine glass.

KEY VOCABULARY

VERBS
arrange
give
introduce
place
put
repeat
serve
take [an order]

NOUNS
à la carte
aperitif
bartender
beverage
coaster
drink
gin
host
menu
order
sherry
stirrer
tonic
waitress

OTHERS
anti-clockwise
clockwise
correct
on the right
ready

FOR SPECIAL ATTENTION

- *beverage* is the general term for any type of drink.
- *aperitif* = French word used in English meaning an alcoholic drink before meals
- *à la carte menu* = menu where items are priced separately. The guest may pick and choose any item from this menu. [*à la carte* is a French term.]
- *clockwise* = move in the same direction as the hands of a clock
- *anti-clockwise* – the opposite direction to the above
- *coaster* = a small mat that is put under a glass to protect the table
- *host/hostess* = the person who invites others to a function or meal

MORE EXPRESSIONS

Picture

1 *"I'm your waitress this evening."*

2 *"This is our à la carte menu, sir."*

3 *"May I take your drinks order now?"*

4 *"What about you, madam?"*

6 *"I'll repeat your order – that's one gin tonic... etc."*

10 *"A gin and tonic for you, madam."*

Clearing Unused Place Settings

1. There were two extra place settings or covers on table 14.

Excuse me. I'll take these away.

2. Holding an empty tray in her left hand, Mary picked up each item of the unused settings...

3. ...and put it on her tray.

I'll be back shortly to take your order.

4. She informed the guests that she would be back soon to take their food order.

5. Mary took the unused cutlery and crockery to the waiter's station.

6. She put each item back in its correct place at the waiter's station.

A Place Setting

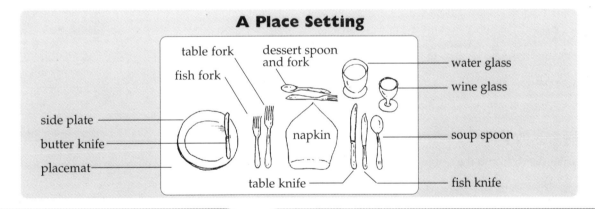

table fork — dessert spoon and fork — water glass — wine glass — fish fork — side plate — butter knife — placemat — napkin — soup spoon — table knife — fish knife

KEY VOCABULARY

VERBS
hold
inform
pick [up]
put [back]
set
take [an order]
take [away]

OTHERS
correct
empty
extra
unused

NOUNS
a set of [something]
cover
crockery
cutlery
flatware
food order
item
placemat
place settings
side plate
silverware
station
tray

FOR SPECIAL ATTENTION

- *set a table* = arrange knives, forks etc. on the table for a meal
- *a set* = a group of similar things e.g. cutlery, a tea set
- *place settings* = a restaurant table is set according to the number of places [chairs] there are at the table.
- *unused* = not in use
- *extra* = more than needed
- The *waiter's station* is an area in the restaurant where items needed at the table are kept.
- *a food order* = the food items that guests would like to have
- *cutlery* = knives, forks, and spoons used for eating and serving food. [US] *flatware, silverware*.
- *crockery* = plates, cups, dishes etc. made from clay

UNIT 3 – Exercises

1. Give one word to describe each group of items pictured below.

1. _a food order_

2. _____

3. _____

4. _____

5. _____

6. _____

2. Find a word in the box that is _opposite_ in meaning to the underlined words in the sentences below. Take care! There are more words in the box than you need.

take away	give	inform	extra	correct	empty
picked up	clockwise	arrange	unused	serve	

E.g. There were _not enough_ chairs at that table.   [_____extra_____]

1. They passed the notice around the table in an _anti-clockwise_ direction.   [_____]

2. The waiters _bring_ the meals to the table.   [_____]

3. It was hard to find the books because they were in the _wrong_ place.   [_____]

4. The waitress _put down_ the tray of cutlery before she set the table.   [_____]

5. On a busy night all the trays are _in use_ by the waiters.   [_____]

6. During the weekend the restaurant is usually _full_.   [_____]

3. Name the object or person in the pictures below.

1. _____

2. _____

3. _____

4. _____

5. _____

6. _____

7. _____

8. _____

4. Match the terms on the left with the statements on the right.

1. Introducing yourself.   [f]   a. "Would you like to order an aperitif?"

2. Repeating an order.   [   ]   b. "Order for table 14."

3. Giving out the menu.   [   ]   c. "I'll be back to take your order."

4. Asking the guests if they want a drink.   [   ]   d. "This is our à la carte menu."

5. Informing the guests about your action.   [   ]   e. "That's one sherry and three gins."

6. Giving the drinks order to the bar.   [   ]   f. "My name is Sarah."

5. What is the waiter saying in these pictures? Complete the dialogue below.

1. Waiter: _____

   Guest: Good evening.

2. Waiter: _____

   Guest: Thank you.

3. Waiter: _____

4. Guest: Yes. A dry sherry, please.

   Waiter: _____

5. Waiter: _____

   Guest: I'll have a gin and tonic, please.

6. Waiter: _____

   Guest: That's right.

6. Role-play the above dialogue with a partner.

May I take your food order now?

1. Mary asked the guests at table 14 if she could take their food order.

The fresh Cape Cod oysters and the Norwegian salmon are our specialities this week.

oysters

salmon

2. She informed the guests about the specialities on the menu for that week.

The oysters to start, and the salmon to follow, please.

Yes, madam.

3. Mary wrote down the details of the order on the Food Order Form.

How would you like your steak, sir? Well-done, medium or rare?

Medium, please.

4. A guest ordered the fillet steak so Mary asked how he wanted his steak cooked.

How are Filets de Sole à la Meuniere prepared?

The sole fillets are sautéd in sweet butter and flavoured with a little lemon juice.

5. Mary had to describe a dish on the menu for another guest.

Mary, is Couscous a vegetable?

No, sir, it's a type of grain made from wheat.

6. She also explained to a guest what a certain ingredient was.

I'll have the asparagus as a starter.

I'm very sorry, sir, but we've run out of asparagus...

7. When a guest asked for something that was no longer available, Mary apologized...

Would you like to try the cucumber mousse instead? It's light and very tasty.

All right. That sounds good.

8. ...and recommended an alternative that was equally light.

Food Order Form

Date 21/3	Table 14	Persons 4	Server Mary

Qty.	Item	
	1st Course	seat numbers
1x	oysters	[1]
1x	mussel salad	[2]
2x	cucumber mousse	[3] [4]
	Main Course	
2x	salmon steak	[1] [3]
1x	fillet steak – medium	[2]
1x	fillet steak – rare	[4]

Note: Dessert orders are usually written on a separate order form.

Would anyone like to order extra vegetables or salad with their main course?

9. She asked if anyone wanted an extra order of vegetables or salad.

May I repeat your order: that's 2 cucumber mousse, 1 oysters, 1 mussel salad...

10. When all the guests had placed their orders, Mary repeated the whole order back to them.

Is that correct?   *Yes, that's right.*

11. Then she asked the guests for confirmation that the order was correct.

KEY VOCABULARY

VERBS
describe
explain
flavour
inform
order
place
recommend
repeat
run out [of]
sauté
to follow
to start

NOUNS
alternative
appetizer
asparagus
cereal
confirmation
dish
entrée
fillet
flavour
food order form
ingredient
main course
meal

mousse
oyster
salad
salmon
sole
specialities
starter
steak
vegetable
wheat

OTHERS
available
equally
fresh
light
medium
rare
tasty
tender
well-done
whole

Thank you. I'll be back soon with your meal.

12. Mary told them she would be back soon with their meal.

FOR SPECIAL ATTENTION

- *specialities* [in restaurants] = certain food items that are freshly made or available on that day or week etc.
- *starter* = another name for the first course of a meal
- The *main course* is the biggest part of the meal, such as meat or fish etc. [Also called the *Entrée* in America.]
- an *alternative* = another choice that is available
- *run out of [something]* = that item is finished or used up and there is no more left
- *Ingredients* are the different food items used to make a certain dish.
- *dish* = a certain type of food. The same word is used for containers for holding or serving food.
- *sauté* = fry quickly in a little oil. [French word used in English.]
- *rare, medium, well-done* = these words are used to describe the way meat is cooked. Meat is rare when it is cooked a very short time.
- *"How would you like your steak done?"* – is one way of asking how you like your steak cooked.
- *light* [food] = food that is easy to digest. Usually a small quantity.

MORE EXPRESSIONS

Picture

1   *"Are you ready to order now?"*
    "Would you like to order now?"

2   *"We have two specialities this week. They are..."*
    "The specialities for this week are ___ and ___."

4   *"How would you like your steak done?"*
    "How do you want your steak cooked?"

7   *"I'm sorry, sir, but there is no more asparagus."*
    "I'm afraid we are out of asparagus, sir."

8   *"I would recommend the cucumber mousse instead."*
    "You may like to try the cucumber mousse instead."

9   *"Would you like any extra vegetables or salad?"*

10 *"I'll repeat the order:..."*

UNIT 4 – Exercises

1. **The sentences in the boxes below tell you what the waiter did when he took a food order. Put his actions into the correct order by giving each box a number.**

[a] He described how the dish was cooked.	[b] He informed them about the restaurant's specialities.	[c] He repeated the whole order back to them.	[d] He recommended another dish to this guest.
[e] He asked the guests if they were ready to order their food.	[f] Another guest asked for salmon for his main course.	[g] A guest wanted to know how a dish was prepared.	[h] He explained that the restaurant had run out of salmon.

2. **Substitute the underlined words in the sentences below with a word from the box. Do not use the same word twice.**

alternative	confirmation	meal	specialities
ingredients	main course	starter	dish

1. He had a good _dinner_ at the restaurant his friend recommended. [_meal_]

2. She served the food on a very pretty _plate_. [_____]

3. That restaurant has _fresh food items_ from different countries on the menu every week. [_____]

4. There were no more oysters so he had to choose an _item that was available_. [_____]

5. For my _first course_ I'll have the mushroom soup. [_____]

6. The chef uses many _different things_ to make that dish. [_____]

7. The _biggest part_ of his meal is usually chicken or fish. [_____]

8. After repeating the whole order to the guests, he asked them _if it was correct_. [for _____]

3. **Match the words in column A with words in column B that are _opposite_ in meaning.**

A	B
1. rare [steak].................. [c]	a. a few days old
2. available...................... [ ]	b. a big meal
3. fresh............................ [ ]	c. well-done
4. tasty............................ [ ]	d. no more left
5. a light dish.................. [ ]	e. not a pleasant flavour

28

4. **What is the waiter saying to the guest? Choose from the sentences given below, and write the number of your choice into the waiter's speech bubbles.**

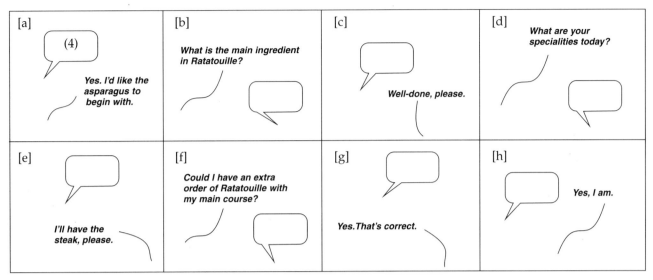

1. "We have some fresh asparagus from Belgium this week."
2. "How would you like your steak done?"
3. "I'll repeat the order: asparagus to start, steak, well-done, and an extra order of Ratatouille. Is that right?"
4. "Are you having a starter, madam?"
5. "Are you ready to order now, madam?"
6. "What would you like for the main course?"
7. "Yes, of course, madam."
8. "Tomatoes, madam, and some other vegetables."

5. **Put the frames in Exercise 4 into the correct order. Rewrite the whole dialogue in the space below. Role play and practise the dialogue with a partner.**

Taking a Food Order

Waiter: *Are you ready to order now, madam?*

Guest: *Yes, I am.*

Correct Order		
1. ___h___	Guest:	_____
2. _____	Waiter:	_____
3. _____	Waiter:	_____
4. _____	Guest:	_____
5. _____	Waiter:	_____
6. _____	Guest:	_____
7. _____	Waiter:	_____
8. _____	Guest:	_____
	Guest:	_____
	Waiter:	_____
	Guest:	_____
	Waiter:	_____
	Waiter:	_____
	Guest:	_____

Placing Food Orders with the Kitchen

There are usually three copies of the Food Order.

For table 14.

1. Mary gave one copy of the food order to the hot kitchen...

2. ...where the hot food is prepared.

Order for table 14.

3. She left the second copy with the cold kitchen for the salads and other cold dishes.

4. She kept the last copy for herself.

5. Mary collected the special knives and forks for steak and fish.

6. She also put a full bread basket and a butter dish on her tray.

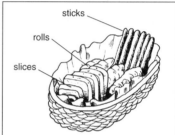

sticks
rolls
slices

7. The bread basket contained rolls, slices and sticks of wholemeal and white bread.

8. At the table, she checked her copy of the food order,...

Excuse me, sir.

9. ...and replaced some of the existing cutlery with steak and fish knives and forks.

10. Mary placed the basket of bread and the butter dish in the centre of the table.

KEY VOCABULARY

VERBS	NOUNS	OTHERS
collect	basket	blunt
contain	bread	cold
keep	butter	existing
leave	centre	flat
place	course	full
prepare	cutlery	hot
replace	dish	sharp
	edge	special
	kitchen	thin
	roll	wholemeal
	shape	
	slice	
	stick	

FOR SPECIAL ATTENTION

- *hot and cold kitchens* – most restaurants prepare hot and cold food in separate kitchens
- A *steak knife* has a very sharp edge to make it easier to cut the meat.
- A *fish knife and fork* have a different shape from the usual cutlery. The knife edge is also more blunt.
- *slice* = a thin, flat piece of something, e.g. bread, cake, meat
- *roll* [bread] = a round piece of bread
- *wholemeal* = flour that is made from the whole grain of wheat including the husk
- *replace* = change one thing for another

1. Mary brought a water jug to the table...

2. ...and topped up the half empty water glasses.

3. She kept one arm behind her back as she worked.

4. A guest was going to smoke a cigarette.

5. Mary took a lighter out of her apron pocket,...

6. ...and lit the cigarette for him.

7. She noticed that the ashtray had more than two cigarette butts in it,...

8. ...so she brought a clean ashtray on a tray to the table.

9. Holding the tray in her left hand, she placed the clean ashtray over the used one,...

10. ...and lifted both ashtrays onto her tray.

11. She then put the clean ashtray back on the table.

★ Restaurant Etiquette

- Stand to the right of guests when removing or placing anything in front of them.
- Say, "Excuse me" if you have to reach across a guest.
- Keep your left arm behind your back while performing any task with your right hand.

KEY VOCABULARY

VERBS	NOUNS	OTHERS
bring	apron	behind
change	arm	clean
hold	ashtray	full
keep	back	half-empty
lift	butt	onto
light	etiquette	over
notice	jug	to the right
perform	lighter	used
reach across	pitcher	
refill	pocket	
remove		
top up		

FOR SPECIAL ATTENTION

- *water jug* = [US] a pitcher of water
- *top up* = fill up a partly empty container
- *cigarette butt* = the short piece that is left of a cigarette after it has been smoked
- *etiquette* = the rules that tell you the correct and polite way to do things
- *stand to the right of someone* = stand on a person's right hand side
- *reach across someone* = stretch your arm in front of the person

31

UNIT 5 – Exercises

1. **All the workers are busy doing something in this restaurant.**
   (A) Choose an action word (verb) from the right that tells you what each worker is doing.
       Write in the verb next to the waiter's number below.
   (B) Make sentences with these verbs.

replacing

lifting

collecting

removing

topping up

placing

bringing

preparing

lighting

reaching across

1. _____ *collecting* _____

   He is collecting glasses from the waiter's station.

2. _____

   _____

3. _____

   _____

4. _____

   _____

5. _____

   _____

6. _____

   _____

7. _____

   _____

8. _____

   _____

9. _____

   _____

10. _____

    _____

32

2. Find the word pairs that are opposites

sharp full right clean

over used left under

blunt behind cold hot

empty round in front of flat

__right / left__   _____   _____   _____

_____   _____   _____   _____

3. Solve the word puzzle with the help of the following clues. Choose from the words below. Take care! You only need ten of the sixteen words.

1. Food is prepared in this place.
2. You wear this over your clothes to keep them clean.
3. This is made from milk. You can spread it on bread.
4. A part of your clothes. You can keep things in this.
5. A container for liquid e.g. milk, water, juice.
6. This produces a small light.
7. The end piece of a cigarette.
8. This type of bread is light brown in colour.
9. You use this when you smoke a cigarette.
10. A thin, flat piece of something.

butter	shape	kitchen	apron	course	jug
slice	basket	lighter	dish	pocket	wholemeal
butt	stick	ashtray	edge		

4. Discuss these questions with your trainer or partner.

1. Why do most restaurants have separate kitchens for preparing hot and cold food?
2. What are some examples of good restaurant etiquette?

This is our wine list, sir.

1. Mary gave the wine list to the host.

There's also a red or white house wine, served by the carafe or glass.

2. She explained about the house wine available by carafe or glass.

We'll have a bottle of Fumé Blanc...

3. The guest made his selection from the wine list,...

... and half a carafe of red, please.

4. ...and also ordered half a carafe of the house red.

5. In the pantry, Mary filled a wine bucket one-third full with ice and a little water.

6. She set up a stand near the table,...

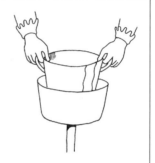

7. ...and placed the wine bucket on the stand.

8. She brought the white wine bottle to the table...

9. ...with the base held on a folded napkin in the palm of her left hand.

The Fumé Blanc, sir.

Yes, that's right.

10. She showed it to the guest with the bottle label facing out.

bulge

foil wrapper

neck

1985 FUMÉ BLANC

11. Then Mary cut the foil wrapper below the bulge on the neck of the bottle.

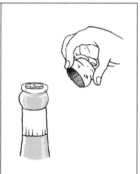

12. She removed the foil and...

13. ...wiped the top of the bottle with the napkin.

14. Mary then pierced the cork with the spiral screw of the wine bottle opener.

15. She held the bottle steady and turned the opener clockwise.

16. The levers of the opener lifted as the screw went into the cork.

17. When the spiral screw was almost at the bottom of the cork...

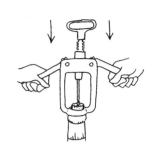

18. ...Mary pressed down the levers and pulled out the cork.

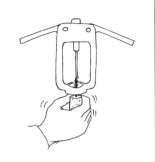

19. She unscrewed the cork from the opener and...

20. ...put it on a side plate beside the host.

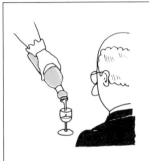

21. She filled the host's wine glass to one-third full...

22. ...and gave the bottle a quarter turn as she lifted it away from the glass.

23. She waited for the host to taste the wine.

Yes, that's fine.

24. When he told her to go ahead,...

Notes about Wine

- There are different types of wine bottle openers.

- Only white and pink wine is kept cold in a wine bucket. Red wine, in a bottle or carafe, is left on the table.

25. ...she began serving the other guests by filling their glasses to three-quarters full.

26. After the guests had been served, Mary left the bottle in the wine bucket.

KEY VOCABULARY

VERBS	NOUNS	OTHERS
begin	bucket	below
bring	bulge	bottom
cut	carafe	folded
explain	cork	one-third
fill	foil	quarter
hold	host	spiral
lift	label	steady
order	lever	three-quarters
pierce	list	
press	neck	
pull out	opener	
remove	palm	
set up	pantry	
show	screw	
taste	selection	
turn	stand	
unscrew	top	
wait	wrapper	
wipe		

FOR SPECIAL ATTENTION

- *host / hostess* – [US] can also be the person in a restaurant who greets guests, shows them to a table etc.
- *house wine* = a wine that is specially selected by the restaurant and sold more cheaply
- *carafe* = a glass container for house wine or water
- *label* = the paper stuck on the bottle that tells you all about the wine
- *house red / white* = the red or white house wine
- *held the bottle steady* = held the bottle so that it didn't move or shake
- *told her to go ahead* = told her to go on and serve the guests
- *...taste the wine...* = the host drinks a little wine to test the flavour. Wine can sometimes turn bad in the unopened bottle.

UNIT 6 – Exercises

1 (A) Choose a verb from the list on the right to describe the action in each picture.

  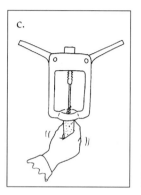 

a. _____ b. _____ c. _____ d. _____

wipe

cut

pierce

remove

unscrew

press down

show

turn
  clockwise

   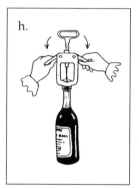

e. _____ f. _____ g. _____ h. _____

(B) Put the above pictures into the correct order for opening a wine bottle, and fill in the blanks below with the letters of the pictures.

The correct order is:

1. _____g_____   2. _____   3. _____   4. _____

5. _____ 6. _____   7. _____   8. _____

2. Cross out the words that do <u>not</u> belong or relate to the categories below.
(NB: There may be more than one word in each category that does not belong.)

(A) Containers for Wine	**(B) Parts of a Wine Bottle Opener**	**(C) Measurements**
1. carafe	1. levers	1. a quarter
2. bowl	2. spiral screw	2. three-quarters
3. bottle	3. label	3. top
4. glass	4. cork	4. one-third

3. Name the parts of a wine bottle.

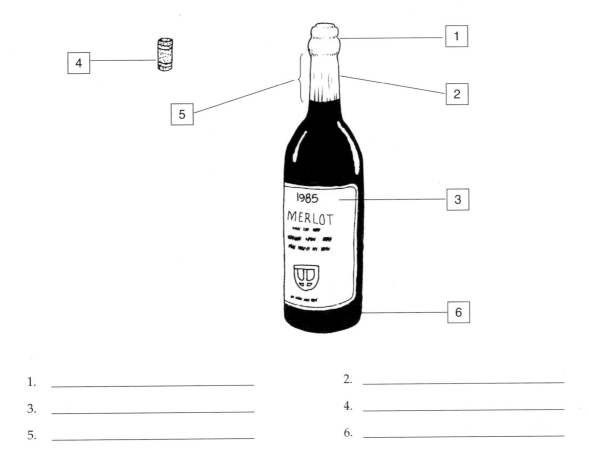

1. _____
2. _____
3. _____
4. _____
5. _____
6. _____

4. Circle the best word for each sentence below.

1. You put the wine bucket on a *table / stand*.

2. You cut the foil wrapper *below / above* the bulge on the neck of the bottle.

3. You pierce the *cork / wrapper* with the bottle opener.

4. You read the *list / label* on the wine bottle.

5. You let the host *drink / taste* the wine before you serve the other guests.

6. You *set up / fill up* a stand for the wine bucket.

7. You *pull out / press down* the cork when you open the bottle.

8. You *fill / serve* the wine-glasses.

9. You *show / hold* the bottle label to the host.

10. You *wipe / remove* the top of the bottle with a napkin.

5. Discuss the following questions with the help of your trainer.

1. Why is the wine bottle cork left beside the host?

2. Why does the waiter give the bottle a quarter turn after he fills a glass?

3. Why is the host's glass only filled to one-third at first?

Serving the First Course / Refilling Wine Glasses

1. Mary saw that the first courses for table 14 were ready.

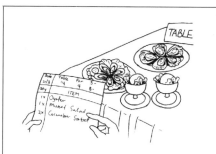

2. She checked the dishes against her food order to make sure they were correct.

3. She then put the plates on a tray...

4. ...and carried the tray to the table using the shoulder carry position.

5. She set the tray down on a tray-stand near table 14,...

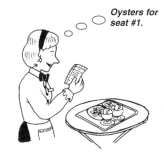

Oysters for seat #1.

6. ...and double-checked the food order, before serving the first guest.

The oysters for you, madam.

7. Mary announced the meal as she put it down in front of the guest.

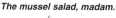

The mussel salad, madam.

8. Next, she served the other ladies at the table.

Your cucumber mousse, sir.

9. The host was served last, after all the other guests had been served.

Carrying a Tray in the Shoulder Carry Position

Fig. 1 Pull the tray so that it projects 15 cm from the edge of the table or tray-stand.

Fig. 2 Slide your left hand under the tray so that your palm is under the heaviest part of the tray.

Fig. 3 Bend your knees and lift the tray off the table.

Fig. 4 Carry the tray at shoulder height. Keep the tray steady with your right hand.

10. Mary noticed that some wine glasses were only a quarter full,...

11. ...so she picked up the bottle of wine from the stand...

12. ...and topped up a glass.

13. Another guest indicated that she did not want more wine.

14. The wine bottle was almost empty,...

Would you care for another bottle, sir? **No, thank you.**

15. ...so Mary asked the host if he wanted another bottle.

16. She put the bottle back into the wine bucket.

When to Start Serving

Make sure **all** the dishes for the course are ready before you start serving.

Order of Service

Without host, serve:

first – all the ladies, in a clockwise direction. Then serve the gentlemen.

With host, [male or female], serve:

first	– lady or gentleman to the right of host
second	– other ladies
third	– gentlemen
last	– host

With host

KEY VOCABULARY

VERBS
announce
bend
care for [something]
double check
indicate
make sure
notice
pick up
project
refill
set down
slide
top up

NOUNS
bucket
edge
female
first course
host
knees
male
palm
position
shoulder

OTHERS
almost
empty
heaviest
ready
steady

FOR SPECIAL ATTENTION

- The *first course* of a meal is sometimes called a *starter*, an *appetizer* or an *entrée*.
  NB: In American-style restaurants the *main* course is often called the *Entrée*.
- *shoulder carry position* = food trays are usually carried in this position. Beverage trays are carried at waist level.
- *host / hostess* = the person [male or female] who invites others to a meal or function
- *indicate* = to let someone know something by a sign. Guests often indicate they do not want more wine by covering the glass with their hand.
- *announce* = to say out loud
- *double check* = check a second time
- *top up* = fill a glass or container that is not completely empty

UNIT 7 – Exercises

1. Choose a preposition from the box to complete the verbs below each picture. Some prepositions are used more than once.

[This exercise includes verbs from previous units.]

up	of	down	out	away	with	from

(a) set __up__ the stand   (b) put _____ the tray   (c) run _____ _____ oysters   (d) take _____ the ashtray

(e) make eye-contact _____   (f) pull _____ the cork   (g) top _____ the glass   (h) made _____ wheat

2. Find one word from the Key Vocabulary list that can replace each underlined phrase in the sentences below.

E.g.   At a restaurant people usually order a _light dish to begin with_ and then the main course.   _____starter_____

1. The _person who invited the others_, ordered two bottles of red wine.   _____

2. The waitress _looked a second time at_ her food order to make sure it was correct.   _____

3. She _called out the name of_ the meal as she served it to the guest.   _____

4. The guest _covered her glass to show_ that she did not want more wine.   _____

5. She _poured some wine into_ the half-empty glasses on the table.   _____

3. Name these parts of the body.

4. _____

5. _____

6. _____

7. _____

1. _____

2. _____

3. _____

40

4. The trainer is telling a waiter how to carry a tray at shoulder height. Put his instructions into the correct order.

(a) Bend your knees.

(b) Pull the tray out about 15 cm from the edge of the table.

(c) Lift the tray to shoulder height.

(d) Keep the tray steady with your right hand.

(e) Slide your left hand under the tray.

The correct order is: 1. _____   2. _____   3. _____   4. _____   5. _____

5. REVISION WORD PUZZLE. This puzzle contains words from Units 1–7. Solve the puzzle with the help of the clues below.

1. The paper that is stuck on a wine bottle.

2. You put this under a glass to protect the table.

3. This person mixes drinks.

4. Any item of food used to prepare a dish.

5. You remove this when you open a wine bottle.

6. You suggest something tasty on the menu.

7. You use this to eat with.

8. This is also called a booking.

9. A general word for hot or cold drinks.

10. Another word for starter [in USA, the main course].

11. An alcoholic drink before dinner.

12. You stir your drink with this.

6. Discuss these questions with your trainer or partner.

1. Why does the waiter double-check the food order before serving the guests?

2. Mary asks the host if he'd like another bottle of wine. Why?

3. Why is it better to wait until all the dishes for the course are ready before you start serving the guests.

Serving the Main Course

Pick up for table 14.

1. Mary went to the hot kitchen to collect the main courses for table 14.

2. She checked the meals against her food order.

3. Then she put the food covers on each plate...

4. ...and arranged them on a tray.

5. She carried the tray to a tray-stand near table 14.

6. She placed a plate in front of the guest,...

Salmon Steak for you, madam.

7. ...and announced the meal as she took off the food cover.

8. Mary adjusted the plate so that the main portion was directly in front of the guest.

9. After all the guests were given their meals,...

10. ...Mary brought a dish of extra vegetables to the table.

11. Holding a serving fork and spoon in her right hand,... [see below]

12. ...she scooped some vegetables from the dish...

Hand Positions for Holding Service Spoon and Fork

Hand / Fingers

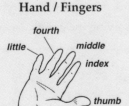

1. Position the spoon at a 45 degree angle so that the handle is **over** the middle and little fingers, and **under** the fourth finger of your right hand.

2. Now hold the fork between the thumb and index finger, **parallel** to the spoon. The base of the handle should be **under** the thumb, and resting against the palm.

3. Pick up food items from the serving dish between the service spoon and fork, and transfer them to the plate.

13. ...and put them to one side on the guest's plate.

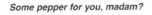

Some pepper for you, madam?

Yes, please.

14. Mary offered freshly ground pepper to the guests.

15. She ground the pepper mill over the food on the plate.

16. She gave a guest some sauce for the salmon steak,...

17. ...and served the salad dressing to another guest.

Could we have more bread, please?

Yes, sir, I'll get some right away.

18. A guest asked Mary for more bread.

19. She brought a full bread basket to the table.

Enjoy your meal.

20. She wished them a good dinner before leaving the table.

Is everything all right?

Very good, thank you.

21. About 15 minutes later, Mary went back to the table to check everything.

22. She continued with other work, but kept an eye on table 14.

The Main Course

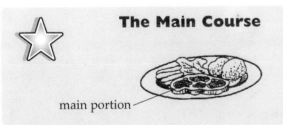

main portion

KEY VOCABULARY

VERBS
adjust
arrange
bring
collect
continue
grind
keep an eye on
offer
scoop
transfer
twist
wish

NOUNS
base
cover
dressing
handle
index finger
meal
oil
pepper mill
plate
portion
sauce
thumb
tray-stand
vinegar

OTHERS
extra
freshly
ground
main
parallel
ready

FOR SPECIAL ATTENTION

- *A pepper mill* contains whole pepper corns.
- *Freshly ground pepper* is made by twisting the top of the pepper mill which grinds the pepper inside to a powder.
- *Sauce* is a thick liquid served with food to add flavour. There are many kinds of sauces.
- *dressing* = a type of sauce especially for salads, usually made from oil and vinegar
- *keep an eye on* = look from time to time to see if all is well

MORE EXPRESSIONS

Picture

18   *I'll bring you some now.*
     I'll be back with some in a minute.

NB: I'll + verb... is an offer to do something for someone.
  e.g.   I'll get you another cup.
       I'll check the Reservation Record.

UNIT 8 – Exercises

1. **Mary is serving the main course. Write in the names of some of the things she serves the guests.**

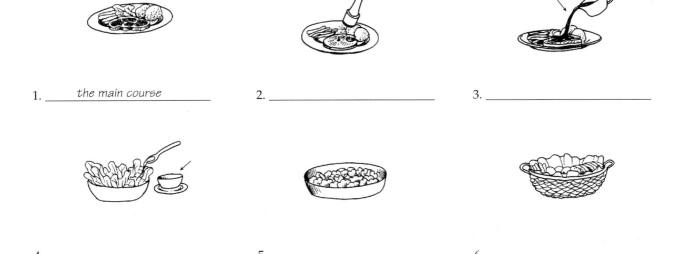

1. _____the main course_____   2. _____   3. _____

4. _____   5. _____   6. _____

2. **(A) The sentences below describe Mary's actions when she served the main course. Pick a verb from the list on the right and fill in the blanks in each sentence.**

(a) She __checked__ the meals against her food order.

(b) She _____ the tray to the table.

(c) She _____ the food cover.

(d) She _____ the meal as she took off the cover.

(e) She _____ food covers on the plates.

(f) She _____ the plates on a tray.

(g) She _____ the tray down on the tray-stand.

(h) She _____ the main courses for table 14.

(i) She _____ freshly ground pepper to the guests.

(j) She _____ the plate in front of the guest.

(k) She _____ the guests a good dinner.

```
carried
took off
wished
offered
placed
arranged
checked
collected
put
set
announced
```

(B) Put the above sentences into the correct order for serving the main course. The correct order is:

1. ___(h)___   2. _____   3. _____   4. _____

5. _____   6. _____   7. _____   8. _____

9. _____   10. _____   11. _____

44

3. Fill in the blanks with the names of the objects in the pictures.

1. She holds the serving fork between her _____

and her _____ finger.

2. She grinds pepper onto the food using a

_____ .

3. She puts food _____ on the plates before

bringing them to the table.

4. She adjusts the plate so that the _____ is in

front of the guest.

5. She puts the heavy tray down on a _____ .

6. She scoops some vegetables from the dish with a

_____ .

7. The _____ of the serving spoon is held

between the fingers of her right hand.

8. Salad dressing is usually made with oil and

_____ .

4. Which of Mary's statements below are offers to do something for the guests? Mark those statements with a ✓ .

1. *"Is everything all right?"*

2. *"I'll find out if the chef can do that for you, sir."*

3. *"I'll get you some bread right away."*

4. *"I'm your waitress this evening."*

5. *"This is our à la carte menu."*

6. *"I'll take your food order in a minute."*

1. Fred was having a hard time! He had to deal with the complaints from some angry customers.

I have a reservation. The name's Dale.

2. First a party of four came in.

I'm sorry, sir, but there's no record of your reservation.

3. Fred apologized when he could not find their name in the reservation record.

But I made a booking for this evening!

4. Fred listened carefully to their complaint.

Could you tell me when you made the reservation, Mr Dale?

Er... I'm not sure.

5. He asked questions to find out the facts.

...but I must have a table tonight!

We are fully booked now, Mr Dale.

6. The guest insisted on a table, so Fred explained the situation,...

...but if you can wait about an hour, I will be able to give you a table.

7. ...and offered him a possible solution,...

You may wish to have a drink at the bar, sir.

All right, then.

8. ...and a place to wait for the table. The guest accepted the solution.

Excuse me!

Yes, sir, can I help you?

9. A guest at table 5 also had a problem.

Look at this steak! I asked for medium, but this is overcooked!

10. He was not satisfied with his steak. Fred listened attentively.

Oh, I'm very sorry, sir.

11. He apologized to the guest,...

I'll inform the chef and get you another steak.

12. ...and offered to replace the steak.

Will that be all right, sir, or would you prefer something else?

Yes, that's fine.

13. He asked for the guest's agreement to the solution.

Table 5 does not want a well-done steak. He asked for medium.

14. Fred took the plate to the kitchen and told the chef the problem.

15. The chef prepared another steak.

I'm sorry about this, sir. Thank you for waiting. I hope this will be all right.

16. Fred took the meal to the table and apologized once again.

Dealing with the Angry Guest

DO NOT!

- Get upset or angry.
- Interrupt the guest.
- Blame others for the problem.
- Blame the guest.
- Argue with the guest.
- Justify the situation.

DO [Follow these steps]

1. Listen attentively.
   [eye-contact; bend to speaker's level].

2. Apologize.

3. Ask questions to find out the facts.

4. Find a solution.

5. Get the guest's agreement to the solution.

6. Solve the problem.

KEY VOCABULARY

VERBS
accept
apologize
argue
be able to
blame
deal with
explain
find out
have [a hard time]
inform
insist
interrupt
justify
listen
offer
prepare
replace
satisfy
solve
suggest

NOUNS
agreement
bar
chef
complaint
fact
question
situation
solution

OTHERS
angry
attentively
carefully
medium
over-cooked
possible
satisfied
tough
upset
well-done

FOR SPECIAL ATTENTION

- *have a hard time* = find yourself in a difficult situation
- *deal with complaints* = try to find a solution to certain problems
- *interrupt someone* = start speaking before the other person can finish what he is saying
- *not satisfied with* = not pleased or happy about something
- *overcooked* = cooked too much
- *ask for agreement* = ask if the person accepts something
- *blame [someone]* = say that someone has done something wrong
- *justify* = give reasons to show that something or somebody is right
- *argue with someone* = express a different opinion from that person in an angry way

MORE EXPRESSIONS

Picture

3   "I'm sorry, sir, but your name is not in the reservation record."

5   "Do you remember when you made the reservation?"

6   "I'm afraid all our tables are full at the moment."

8   "Would you like to have a drink at the bar, sir?"

12   "Could I get you another steak or would you like something else?"

16   "I'm very sorry you had this problem. I hope this steak will be all right."

UNIT 9 – Exercises

1. **Some of the guests at this restaurant have complaints. How does the waiter offer to solve the problems? Match the number of the guest with each solution below.**

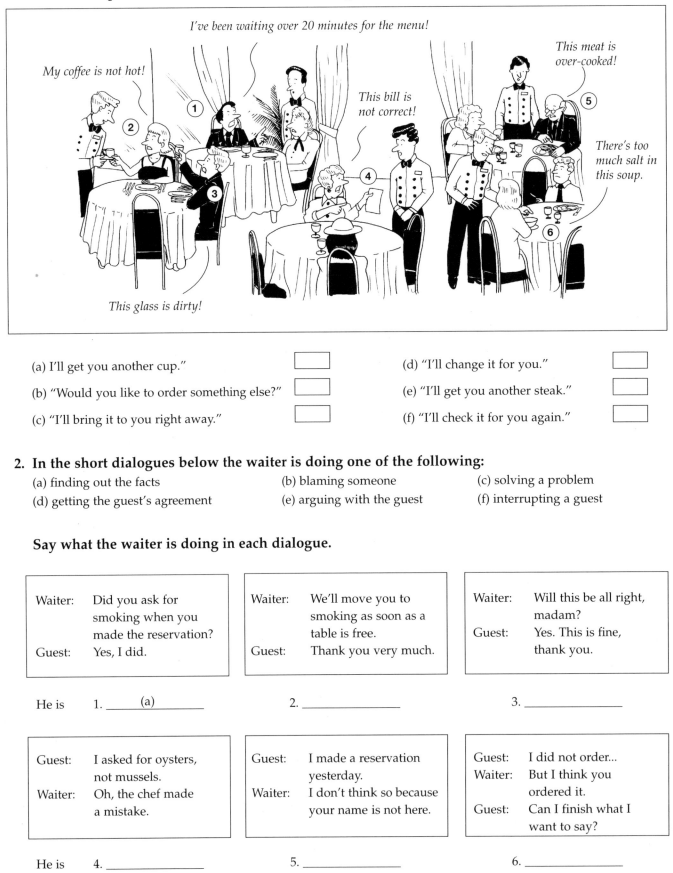

(a) I'll get you another cup." ☐   (d) "I'll change it for you." ☐

(b) "Would you like to order something else?" ☐   (e) "I'll get you another steak." ☐

(c) "I'll bring it to you right away." ☐   (f) "I'll check it for you again." ☐

2. **In the short dialogues below the waiter is doing one of the following:**

(a) finding out the facts   (b) blaming someone   (c) solving a problem
(d) getting the guest's agreement (e) arguing with the guest   (f) interrupting a guest

Say what the waiter is doing in each dialogue.

Waiter:	Did you ask for smoking when you made the reservation?
Guest:	Yes, I did.

Waiter:	We'll move you to smoking as soon as a table is free.
Guest:	Thank you very much.

Waiter:	Will this be all right, madam?
Guest:	Yes. This is fine, thank you.

He is   1. ___(a)___   2. _____   3. _____

Guest:	I asked for oysters, not mussels.
Waiter:	Oh, the chef made a mistake.

Guest:	I made a reservation yesterday.
Waiter:	I don't think so because your name is not here.

Guest:	I did not order...
Waiter:	But I think you ordered it.
Guest:	Can I finish what I want to say?

He is   4. _____   5. _____   6. _____

3. Read the two dialogues below carefully.

Dialogue 1	Dialogue 2
Guest: I'd like a table for four, please.	**Guest:** This meat is very tough. I can't even cut it!
Waitress: Sorry, the restaurant is full. We have no more tables.	**Waitress:** That's not possible, sir. We serve the best quality beef from New Zealand.
Guest: But I have a reservation.	**Guest:** Then maybe it's over-cooked.
Waitress: Name, please.	**Waitress:** I don't think so, sir. We have a very good chef.
Guest: Collins. C-O-L-L-I-N-S.	**Guest:** Look here, I can't eat this steak. What are you going to do about it?
Waitress: Your name is not on the reservation list, sir.	**Waitress:** I'm sorry, but we never have complaints about our food.
Guest: But I called yesterday.	
Waitress: Sorry, I can't help you. We are fully booked tonight.	

(A) Say whether the following statements about Dialogues 1 and 2 are true or false. Put a T or F in the box next to the statement.

Dialogue 1

1. The guest said he made a reservation. ☐

2. The restaurant had some empty tables. ☐

3. The waiter found out the facts. ☐

4. The waiter tried to find a solution to the problem. ☐

5. The waiter was polite but not helpful. ☐

Dialogue 2

1. The guest was wrong to complain. ☐

2. The waiter was polite and correct. ☐

3. He apologized to the guest. ☐

4. He argued with the guest. ☐

5. He did not find a solution to the problem. ☐

(B) Work in pairs. Use more paper and rewrite the above dialogues so that the waitress follows the *correct* steps for dealing with complaints. Role-play the dialogues you have written with your partner.

4. Discuss the following topics and questions with your trainer and colleagues.

1. (a) Describe a complaint from a guest that you had to deal with.

   (b) How did you solve the problem?

2. When should you refer the problem to the manager?

3. What should you do if the guest is clearly wrong?

Clearing the Tables after Courses

1. The guests at table 14 had finished their main course.

Excuse me.
May I clear the table?

2. Mary asked if she could clear the table.

3. She put an empty tray on the tray-stand.

Excuse me.

4. From the guest's right, she first moved the cutlery to the left of his dinner plate.

5. Then she picked up the plate with her right hand,...

6. ...and transferred it to her left hand.

7. She gripped the cutlery firmly under her left thumb.

8. Next, Mary picked up the side plate and any unused cutlery.

9. She took all these items to the tray on the tray-stand.

10. She then cleared the empty wine glasses from the place settings.

11. Mary left the water glasses and any filled wine glasses on the table.

12. She scraped food left on the plates onto one plate before...

When to Clear the Table

- **Do not clear the table until all guests have finished eating.**
  (For tables of eight or more, you may start clearing when most of the guests have finished the course.)

- **Make sure the tray-stand is not directly within the guests' view.**

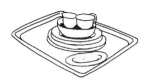

13. ...stacking up the dishes on her tray.

14. When the tray was full, she took it to the clearing station.

15. She brought an empty tray back to continue with the clearing.

16. Finally, she removed the bread basket, butter dish,...

Excuse me, please.

This is our Dessert Menu.

I'll be back shortly to take your order.

17. ...and the salt and pepper shakers from the centre of the table.

18. Mary gave the dessert menu to the guests.

19. She left the table to give the guests some time to study the menu.

SCRAPE off food from plates as quietly as possible.

STACK dishes with the largest and heaviest on the bottom.

FOR SPECIAL ATTENTION

- *clear the table* = remove all the dirty and used dishes and cutlery from the table
- *clearing station* – dirty dishes, etc. are taken from the tables and left in this area of the restaurant. From here, other staff [*stewards*], take the dishes away to be washed.
- *salt and pepper shakers* = these are containers for salt and pepper, which are kept on every table during a meal
- *...not directly within the guests' view...* = not be in a position where guests can see clearly what the waiter is doing

KEY VOCABULARY

VERBS	NOUNS	OTHERS
clear	bread basket	bottom
continue	butter dish	directly
finish	clearing station	empty
grip	cutlery	filled
move	plate	finally
remove	shakers	firmly
scrape	steward	first
stack	view	heaviest
study		largest
transfer		next
		then
		unused

The Dessert Menu

Some restaurants have a separate menu for desserts. In others, desserts are included in the à la carte menu.

UNIT 10 – Exercises

NB: Vocabulary items from previous units may be included in the following exercises.

1. **Find the word pairs that are opposites.**

Heaviest   top   bottom   firstly   unused   over   under   finally   dirty   leave   arrive   smalliest   lightest   largest   Satisfied   upset

firstly / finally   _____   _____   _____

_____   _____   _____   _____

2. **Replace the underlined words in each sentence with a word from the box that is closest in meaning.**

heaviest	transferred	stacked	study	scrape
clearing station	cleared	finally	largest	grip

1. When they had finished their meal, the waitress <u>took away all the dirty dishes from</u> the table. _____

2. The big dishes are usually the <u>ones that weigh the most</u>. _____

3. <u>Keep a strong hold of</u> the knife and fork so that they do not fall off the plate. _____

4. She used a fork to <u>push bits of food from</u> the plate before putting it on the tray. _____

5. After the plates were <u>placed on top of one another</u>, they were taken to the kitchen. _____

6. Guests like to <u>go through all the items on</u> the menu before making their selection. _____

7. The waiters take the dirty dishes to the <u>special area in the restaurant</u> and leave them there. _____

8. <u>After everything was cleared</u>, she brought the dessert menu to the table. _____

9. The <u>biggest sized</u> dishes on the table were the dinner plates. _____

10. She <u>changed the position of</u> the plate from her right hand to her left hand. _____

3. Name the items in the centre of this table.

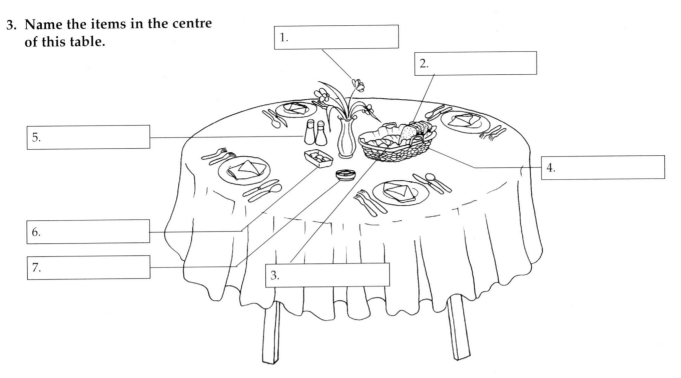

1.

2.

5.

4.

6.

7.

3.

4. REVIEW OF EXPRESSIONS! (Units 1–10)

Match the terms on the left with the statements on the right.

1. recommending something — d

2. apologizing

3. announcing a dish

4. saying something is not available

5. asking about something

6. offering something

7. asking how the guest wants something cooked

8. repeating an order back to the guest

9. asking for agreement to something

10. describing how a dish is made

11. offering to do something for someone

12. describing the ingredients in a dish

(a) "Your rack of lamb, sir."

(b) "That's one green salad, one mush-room soup and two sirloin steaks."

(c) "I'm very sorry, madam, but we're fully booked."

(d) "You may like the salmon mousse. It's our speciality."

(e) "I'll ask the chef to prepare your meal with less salt."

(f) "Which section would you like – smoking or non-smoking?"

(g) "I'm afraid we've run out of smoked salmon."

(h) "It's first marinated in herbs, then grilled over charcoal."

(i) "Moussaka is made from minced lamb, tomato puree and aubergines."

(j) "Will that be all right, sir?"

(k) "More coffee for you, madam?"

(l) "How would you like your steak done?"

Serving Dessert / Making Coffee

Serving Dessert

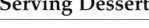

May I take your dessert order now?

Just an espresso for me.

The chocolate mousse, please.

1. Mary asked the guests at table 14 if they were ready to order dessert.

2. She wrote down the orders for dessert and coffee on the dessert order form.

What about you, madam? Our home-made ice-creams are very good.

Okay, I'll try the lychee sorbet.

3. She suggested the house speciality to one of the guests.

4. After Mary had taken the whole order, she gave one copy to the cold kitchen.

5. As soon as the desserts were ready, she put them on a tray,...

6. ...and took them immediately to the table so that the ice-cream orders did not melt.

The sorbet for you, madam.

7. She served the desserts in the usual order,...

Enjoy your desserts. I'll be back with the coffee.

8. ...and then went to the pantry to prepare the hot beverages.

The Dessert Trolley

Some restaurants display non-frozen desserts like cakes and tarts on a dessert trolley. The trolley is brought to the table for guests to make their selection.

cake

tart

KEY VOCABULARY

VERBS
display
melt
prepare
suggest

NOUNS
cake
dessert
mousse
pantry
sorbet

speciality
tart
trolley

OTHERS
immediately
non-frozen
usual

FOR SPECIAL ATTENTION

- *house speciality* = a food item for which the restaurant is well-known
- *mousse* – the main ingredients of this dish are cream and eggs
- *sorbet* = a frozen dessert made of fruits, sugar and water
- *trolley* = a small table on wheels. Also called a *cart*.
- *pantry* = a small room where food or food related items are kept

MORE EXPRESSIONS

Picture

1 *"Are you ready to order dessert now?"*

3 *"I recommend our home-made ice-creams."*
   "Would you like to try our home-made ice-creams?"

7 *"Your lychee sorbet, madam."*

Making Coffee

1. The coffee machine and other equipment for making hot drinks are kept in the pantry.

2. At Chez Max, this machine makes different kinds of coffee.

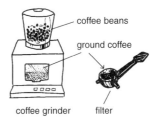

coffee beans
ground coffee
coffee grinder   filter

3. To make two cups of cappuccino, Mary first filled the filter with ground coffee.

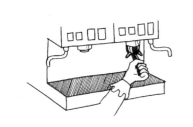

4. Then she attached the filter to the machine...

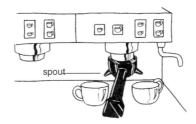

spout

5. ...and put cups under the two spouts on the filter.

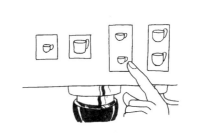

6. She pressed the button for two cups of strong coffee.

7. The machine dispensed coffee into the cups.

nozzle

8. She then put a jug containing cold milk under the nozzle.

9. She let the steam froth up the milk.

10. She poured the milk and froth into the cups and...

11. ...sprinkled on some powdered chocolate.

single spout
demitasse

12. To make one cup of espresso, Mary used a single-spout filter and a *demitasse*.

13. She attached the filter to the machine and pressed the correct button.

saucer   teaspoon

14. She placed all the cups on the right sized saucers with teaspoons.

Coffee machines may be a little different from the one above. The process of making coffee is the same.

KEY VOCABULARY

VERBS	NOUNS		OTHERS
attach	button	jug	powdered
dispense	demitasse	nozzle	single
fill	equipment	saucer	strong
froth up	filter	spout	under
pour	froth	steam	
press	grinder	teaspoon	
sprinkle	ground coffee		

FOR SPECIAL ATTENTION

- *strong* [coffee] = coffee that has more flavour or taste
- *espresso* = a strong coffee that is usually drunk without milk
- *cappuccino* = coffee served with milk that is made frothy by steam
- *froth* [milk] = milk that contains many small bubbles
- *demitasse* = a French word meaning a half-sized cup. Espresso coffee is served in a demitasse.
- *coffee grinder* = a machine that grinds coffee beans into a powder

UNIT 11 – Exercises

1. Name the objects in the pictures below.

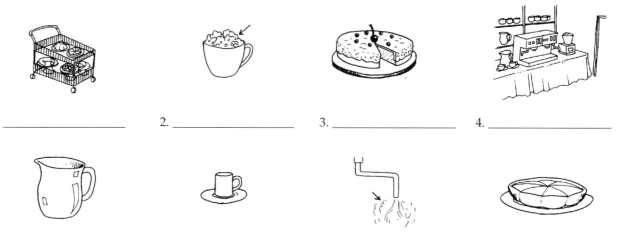

1. _____ 2. _____ 3. _____ 4. _____

5. _____ 6. _____ 7. _____ 8. _____

2. Fill in the blanks in the sentences below with words that describe the actions shown in the pictures. Choose from the verbs given on the right.

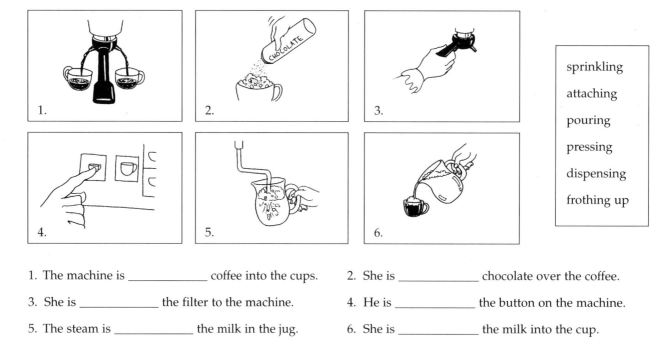

sprinkling

attaching

pouring

pressing

dispensing

frothing up

1. The machine is _____ coffee into the cups.   2. She is _____ chocolate over the coffee.

3. She is _____ the filter to the machine.   4. He is _____ the button on the machine.

5. The steam is _____ the milk in the jug.   6. She is _____ the milk into the cup.

3. All the items below are used to make coffee. Write the name of the item in the space provided.

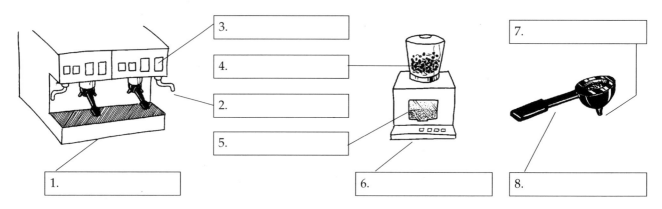

3. _____

4. _____

2. _____

5. _____

7. _____

1. _____   6. _____   8. _____

4. **Which term best <u>explains</u> the underlined word in each sentence below? Mark your choice with a ✓.**

1. He asked the waiter for a cup of **strong** coffee.

   (a) hard

   (b) coffee with milk

   (c) coffee with a lot of flavour / taste

   (d) heavy

2. Take the ice-cream **immediately** to the table.

   (a) at once

   (b) as soon as possible

   (c) later

   (d) in a few minutes

3. Ice-cream **melts** quickly after it is served.

   (a) becomes cool

   (b) turns into liquid

   (c) stays soft

   (d) tastes good

4. Cakes and tarts are **non-frozen** desserts.

   (a) not very cold

   (b) sweet and cold

   (c) not kept cold and hard in the freezer

   (d) cool

5. That restaurant **displays** some dishes in the window.

   (a) shows what they look like

   (b) tells guests about them

   (c) describes them

   (d) puts them in order

6. I like **desserts**.

   (a) places with few trees or plants

   (b) chocolate mousse

   (c) cakes or tarts

   (d) a sweet dish eaten at the end of a meal

5. **The waiter is taking an order for dessert and coffee. Put the statements of the waiter and the two guests into a dialogue. Role play the dialogue with a partner.**

Waiter: _____ *Would you like any desserts?* _____

Guest: _____ *Yes, I'd like the apple tart, please.* _____

_____

_____

_____

_____

_____

_____

_____

_____

_____

_____

_____

_____

_____

_____

Guests 1 and 2
"Just coffee for me."
"Yes, I'd like the apple tart, please."
"An espresso, please."
"No dessert for me, thank you. I've eaten too much."
"Yes, I'll have a cappuccino."

Waiter
"What sort of coffee would you like, sir?"
"Certainly, madam. What about you, sir?"
"Would you like any desserts?"
"Would you like to try our fruit tarts, sir? They are the house specialities."
"Any coffee for you, madam?"

Making Tea / Serving Beverages after Meals

1. To make a cup of tea, Mary first warmed a teapot.

2. Then she put a teabag into the warm teapot...

3. ...and filled the pot three-quarters full with boiling water.

4. Mary put the prepared coffee, the teapot, and an empty cup and saucer on a tray.

5. She also put a sugar bowl and a milk jug on the tray.

6. The sugar bowl contained sachets of different kinds of sugar.

7. Mary carried the beverage tray in the waist-carry position to the tray-stand.

Excuse me, please.

8. First, she placed the milk jug and sugar bowl in the centre of the table.

9. Then she set the empty cup and saucer down in front of the first guest...

Tea for you, madam.

10. ...and filled the cup three-quarters full of tea.

11. She left the teapot on the table to the right of the guest.

Your Cappuccino, madam.

12. She served the next two guests their cappuccinos...

Espresso, sir

13. ...and gave the demitasse of espresso to another guest.

Some Hot Beverages

COFFEES	OTHER
Instant coffee	Tea
Brewed coffee	Herbal teas
Café Mocha	Hot Chocolate
Café Latte	Milk
Cappuccino	
Espresso	

Would you like any liqueurs or brandy?

14. Mary asked if anyone wanted an after-dinner drink.

Yes, a Cognac, VSOP, please.

A Cointreau, please.

15. A guest ordered a brandy...

16. ...and another wanted a liqueur.

Order for table 14.

17. Mary took the order to the bar.

18. The bartender poured some cognac into a brandy snifter.

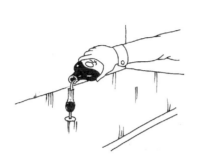

19. He filled a liqueur glass with Cointreau.

20. Mary carried the drinks to the table on a small service plate.

Cognac, sir

21. She served the guests their drinks.

Is there anything else I can get you?

No. Thank you very much.

22. She checked if the guests needed anything else.

23. Then she left to continue her work at another table.

KEY VOCABULARY

VERBS
brew
bring
carry
contain
continue
filter
order
pour
set [down]
stir
want
warm

OTHERS
boiling
brewed
empty
herbal
instant
prepared

NOUNS
bar
bartender
bowl
brandy
creamer
forearm
liqueur
sachet
snifter
stem
sweetener
tea-bag
tea-leaves
teapot

FOR SPECIAL ATTENTION

- *she warmed the teapot* – she put a little hot water into the pot to make it warm. When the pot was warm, she poured away the water.
- *sweetener* – a substance that is used instead of sugar to make food and drink sweet.
- **milk jug** = [US] creamer
- *waist-carry position* – the beverage tray rests on the forearm and open palm and is carried at waist level
- *instant coffee* – this coffee is made quickly just by stirring in hot milk or water to the coffee powder
- *brew* [tea or coffee] – leave coffee or teabags / tea-leaves in boiling water for a few minutes
- *brewed coffee* – boiling water is added slowly to ground coffee and filtered before the coffee is ready for drinking
- *Herbal teas* are not made from tea-leaves but from leaves of special plants known as herbs, e.g. mint, camomile etc.
- *brandy* = a strong alcoholic drink made from grapes or other fruits
- *liqueur* = a strong, sweet alcoholic drink made from different fruits and usually drunk only after meals
- *An after-dinner drink* is usually either a liqueur or a brandy.
- *snifter* = a bowl-shaped glass on a stem. Brandy is always served in this type of glass.

UNIT 12 – Exercises

1. **Name all the items on Mary's tray.**

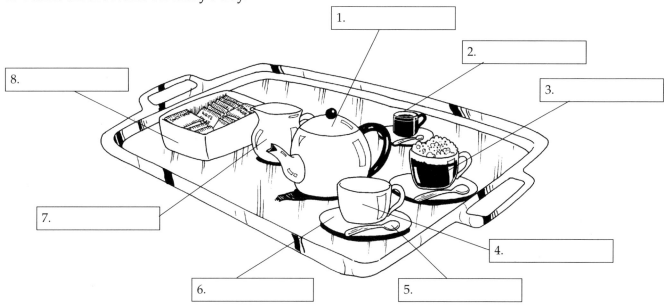

1. _____
2. _____
3. _____
4. _____
5. _____
6. _____
7. _____
8. _____

2. **Describe how you make a cup of tea. Fill in the blanks with the words in the box. There is one word for each blank.**

teapot	pour out	boiling	sugar	water	tea-leaves
brew	three-quarters	teabag	putting	warm	teacup

Making a Cup of Tea

First, (1) _____ a small teapot by (2) _____ a little hot water into it. When the (3) _____ is warm,

(4) _____ the water. Then put a (5) _____ or two teaspoons of (6) _____ into the warmed teapot.

Fill the teapot (7) _____ full with (8) _____ water. Let the tea (9) _____ for a few minutes.

Serve the tea in a (10) _____ and saucer, with milk and (11) _____ or a slice of lemon.

3. **The sentences on the right are clues to the words on the left. Match the words with their clues.**

A

1. stem.............................[c]
2. instant coffee..............[   ]
3. herbal tea....................[   ]
4. sweetener....................[   ]
5. snifter.........................[   ]
6. brewed coffee.............[   ]
7. liqueur........................[   ]
8. brandy.........................[   ]

B

a. This is served in a very small glass.

b. This glass is shaped like a bowl.

c. You hold this part of a wine glass when you are drinking from it.

d. Coffee made by slowly dripping hot water through ground coffee.

e. This coffee is quick and easy to make.

f. This is a strong alcoholic drink made from grapes or fruit.

g. This is made with the leaves of certain plants.

h. People sometimes use this in their coffee or tea.

4. **Who is the person at the bar, and what drinks has he just poured?**
   Write your answers in the spaces provided.

7. [   ]

4. [   ]

6. [   ]

5. [   ]

3. [   ]

2. [   ]

1. [   ]

5. **Practise ASKING.**
   Use the question forms below and practise asking guests if they want the items on the right.

e.g.

Could I get you

Would you like

another cup of coffee?   another cup of

1. _____ ?
   _____ ? }   an after dinner drink

2. _____ ?
   _____ ? }   some / more

3. _____ ?
   _____ ? }   a

4. _____ ?
   _____ ? }   a glass of

5. _____ ?
   _____ ? }   anything else

6. **Discuss these questions with your trainer.**

   1. Why do some people use a sweetener in their drinks?

   2. Why are liqueurs and brandies served in special sized and shaped glasses?

7. **Learn the names of some well-known liqueurs and brandies.**

Could we have the check, please?

Yes, sir. I'll get it for you right away.

1. The guests at table 14 asked for their check.

Check for table 14, please.

2. Mary went to the cashier and asked for the check for table 14.

3. She went through the check to see if all items were included and correct.

4. She put a pen and the check in a check-holder...

5. ...and put the check-holder on a service plate.

Excuse me. Your check, sir.

6. At the table, she placed the closed check-holder in front of the host.

7. Mary stood a little distance away while the guest examined the bill.

Do you take Maxicard?

Yes, we do, sir.

8. He wished to pay by credit card.

9. Mary put his credit card in the check-holder...

Tips

- Some guests include a tip for the waiter on their credit card payment voucher.

- Others leave a cash tip on the table.

Sample of a Credit Card Voucher

ALPSBANK

GEORGE RESTAURANT
Lot 123, Jln 18/25, Las Vegas
United State of America

4565430034
000000007689324

- - - - - - - - - - - - - - - - -

MAXICARD
1609 1234 7623 7689
JAYA LENO

SALE
000987   06/99
25DEC99   009876
123456431   12:45
                3456543

AMOUNT :   250.90

- - - - - - - - - - - - - -

TOTAL :   250.90

Cardmember signature
X

10. ...and gave it to the cashier for processing.

Please sign here, sir.

11. After the card was processed, Mary brought it back to the guest for signing.

12. Mary verified the guest's signature against the card.

13. The two signatures looked the same.

Your card, sir.

14. She then returned the credit card to the guest.

This is your copy, sir.

15. She also gave him the customer's copy of the credit card vouchers...

16. ...and a copy of the check.

17. The guests left a tip on the table.

Thank you for dining with us...

18. As they stood up to leave, Mary thanked them...

Goodbye, sir, goodnight, madam. Hope to see you again soon.

19. ...and said goodbye.

A Cash Payment

A guest places the cash in the check-holder.

Take the cash to the cashier.

Put any change into the check-holder and take it to the guest.

KEY VOCABULARY

VERBS
examine
go [through]
include
pay
present
process
return
sign
verify
wish

OTHERS
closed
correct
included

NOUNS
bill
cash
cashier
change
check
check-holder
copy
credit card
customer
payment
processing
signature
statement
tip
voucher

FOR SPECIAL ATTENTION

- *process a credit card* = take certain actions to make sure the card can be used, etc.
- *check* − a statement of the money that has to be paid for something. Also called a *bill*.
- *verify something* = make sure something is accurate or true
- *tip* = a special sum of money given to waiters, taxi-drivers etc. for their service
- *change* = the money returned to someone when the cost of something is less than the amount given by that person as payment

MORE EXPRESSIONS

Picture

11	*"Could you sign here, please?"*
14	*"Here's your card, sir."*
18	*"Thank you. I hope you enjoyed your dinner."*
19	*"I hope we'll see you again soon."*

UNIT 13 – Exercises

1. Find a word for each picture below.

1. _____

2. _____

3. _____

4. _____

5. _____

6. _____

2. Choose a word from the box that describes the action in each picture.

asked	processed	included	took
signed	examined	gave	verified

(a)

He _____ the
check.

(b)

The guest _____
a tip for the waiter.

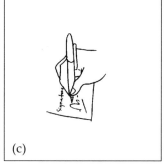

(c)

He _____ the
payment voucher.

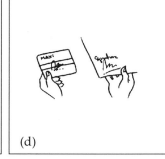

(d)

She _____ the
signature.

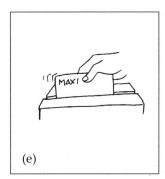

(e)

The cashier _____
the credit card.

(f)

He _____ for
his check.

(g)

He _____ his
credit card to the
waitress.

(h)

She _____ the
credit card to the
cashier.

3. What is the correct order of the above actions? List the letters of the pictures in order from 1 – 8.

1. _(f)_   2._____   3._____   4._____   5._____   6._____   7._____   8._____

4. Say if the following sentences are true or false.
Write T or F in the answer box after each sentence.

1. Guests usually do not leave a tip for the waiter if the service is bad. ☐

2. The check-holder is left open when it is presented to the guest. ☐

3. Mary waited close to the guest while he went through the check. ☐

4. The customer's copy of the credit card vouchers is given to the guest. ☐

5. Mary looked at the signature on the credit card to see if it was the same as the guest's signature. ☐

6. The cashier must make sure that the credit card can be used. ☐

7. The credit card must be returned to the guest. ☐

8. The cashier goes through the bill to make sure that all items ordered by the guest are included. ☐

5. (a) Match the dialogue balloons of the waitress and the guest.

Waitress

Thank you very much, sir.
Thank you, madam. Goodnight.
1 – (E)

Can I get you
anything else?
2 – (   )

We hope to see
you again soon.
3 – (   )

Here's your card, sir, and
your copy of the voucher.
4 – (   )

I hope you enjoyed your dinner.
5 – (   )

Guest

Yes, we did. It was a
very good meal.
A

No, thank you.
We are leaving now.
B

We'll certainly come again.
C

Thank you.
D

Goodnight.
E

(b) Write the above dialogue out in the correct order, and role-play it with your partner.

Waitress: _Here's your card, sir, and your copy of the voucher._ _____

Guest: _____

_____

_____

_____

_____

_____

_____

_____

_____

1. Mary went to the pantry to get some glasses for the table.

2. She noticed a crack on one glass.

3. The rim of another glass was chipped.

broken   cracked   chipped

4. She put these glasses into the discard bin.

5. Another glass with a lipstick stain on it needed to be washed again.

6. Some glasses had lint or water spots on them.

7. To polish these glasses, Mary filled a basin with very hot water.

8. Then she held a stained glass over the steam.

9. The steam moistened the glass.

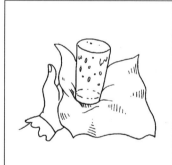

10. She placed the wet glass on a clean cloth in one hand...

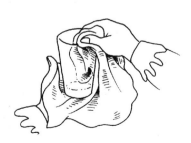

11. ...and inserted the edge of the cloth into the glass with the other hand.

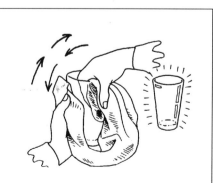

12. She rotated the glass until it was polished and sparkling.

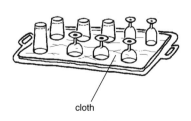

cloth

13. Mary put the spotless glasses face down on a lined service tray.

14. She positioned the stems of some wine glasses between her fingers so that...

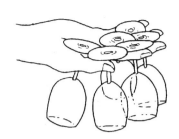

15. ...the base of each glass overlapped the next...

16. ...and took them to the table.

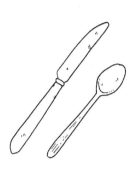

17. Mary noticed that some cutlery looked dull.

18. She got a clean cloth, and polished it...

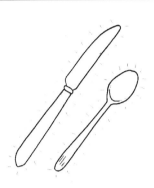

19. ...until it was bright and shiny.

VERBS
discard
handle
hold
insert
moisten
need
notice
overlap
polish
position
rotate
wash

NOUNS
base
basin
bin
bottom
chip
cloth
crack
edge
glassware
lint
lipstick
mark
pantry
rim
smudge
stain
steam
stem
water spot

OTHERS
between
bright
broken
chipped
clean
cracked
dull
face-down
lined
polished
shiny
smudged
sparkling
spotless
stained

20. She saw a finger-print smudge on a knife,...

21. ...so she wiped off the mark with the polishing cloth.

FOR SPECIAL ATTENTION

- *chipped* [glass or crockery] – a glass or plate etc. which has a small piece broken off from its edge or rim
- *cracked* [glass etc.] – a glass etc. that shows a line along which it has broken. The item is still in one piece.
- *broken* [glass etc.] – the item is damaged and in pieces
- *lint* = dust-like bits of fabric that cloth sometimes leaves on glasses
- *water spot* = a stain that water sometimes makes when it dries on a surface
- *lipstick stain* = a stain on a glass made when someone wearing lipstick drinks from the glass
- *discard bin* – a container for broken, chipped or cracked items
- *lined service tray* = a tray that has a clean cloth on it
- *face down* = upside down
- *rotate* = turn something in a circular direction

UNIT 14 – Exercises

1. Find all the words in the box that tell you what is <u>wrong</u> with glassware or cutlery.

heavy	stained	broken	strong	loud	dirty
rude	cracked	long	large	chipped	smudged

_____   _____   _____

_____   _____   _____

2. Match the words you have chosen above with the pictures below.

1.   _____

2.   _____

3.   _____

4.   _____

5.   _____

6.   _____

3. Put a ✓ next to the words that describe glassware or cutlery which is <u>ready to be used</u>.

1. spotless

2. bright

3. soft

4. polished

5. smooth

6. shiny

7. sharp

8. sparkling

9. round

10. pleasant

4. Choose the right word from the list on the right and fill in the blanks below.

1. He _____ a fork into the meat to see if the meat was cooked.

2. She positioned some wine glasses between her fingers so that the base of each glass _____ the next.

3. To polish a glass, you must hold the glass on a cloth and _____ it against the cloth.

4. The tray was _____ with a cloth to protect the glasses.

5. Glasses are placed _____ on a tray to protect them from dust.

6. When the head-waiter passed the table he _____ that the guests did not have a menu.

notice
rotate
inserted
face down
lined
overlapped

5. Pick a word from the box for each blank in the passage below.

smudges	rim	lipstick stain	polishing	fingerprint	hold	chip
lint	moistened	polish	handle	water-spots	steam	base
between	dull	basin	discard bin	face-down	washed	

The restaurant manager was very angry! When he inspected the tables, he found a glass which had a 1. _____

on it. That glass had to be 2. _____ again. Another glass had many 3. _____ on it, and two other glasses

had 4. _____ on them. He made a waiter 5. _____ these glasses over a 6. _____ of hot water.

The 7. _____ from the water 8. _____ the glasses. Then the waiter had to 9. _____ the glasses until

they were spotless and sparkling. The manager became really angry when he saw a glass that had a 10. _____

on its 11. _____ . He told one of the waiters to put this glass into the 12. _____ . He also saw some cutlery

that was 13. _____ and needed 14. _____ . He instructed the waiters to 15. _____ cutlery carefully so

that there would be no 16. _____ 17. _____ on it. The manager also reminded the waiters to hold a wine

glass by its 18. _____ or stem when placing it on the table. The glasses are carried to the tables 19. _____

on a tray or with their stems positioned 20. _____ the waiter's fingers.

69

Setting the Table

1. There were some crumbs on the tablecloth.

2. Mary held a service plate just under the edge of the table...

3. ...and with a folded napkin, she brushed the crumbs off the table onto the plate.

4. She then put the glasses, flatware, china, and other items she needed in the middle of the table.

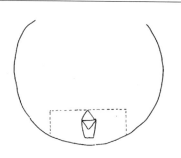

5. First, Mary placed a napkin in the middle of the place setting...

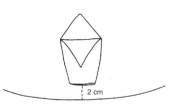

6. ...about 2 cm from the bottom edge of the table.

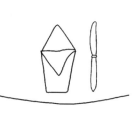

7. Then she placed the table knife on the right, 4 cm from the napkin.

8. She put a fish knife next to the table knife.

9. She positioned a soup spoon next to the fish knife.

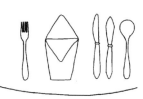

10. She set a table fork down 4 cm to the left of the napkin...

11. ...and placed a fish fork on the outer side of it.

12. Mary made sure that all the flatware was in line with the napkin.

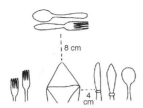

13. She placed a dessert spoon and fork about 8 cm above the napkin.

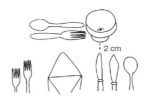

14. She positioned a water goblet about 2 cm above the tip of the table knife.

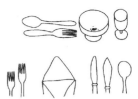

15. Then she placed a wine glass on the right of the water goblet.

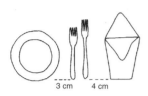

16. Next, Mary put a side plate on the left, about 3 cm from the fish fork.

17. She placed a butter knife on the right side of the side plate.

18. She then arranged a small vase of flowers in the centre of the table.

19. Finally, Mary put an ashtray and the pepper and salt shakers in the middle of the table.

20. The tablecloth on the next table was soiled...

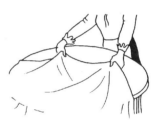

21. ...so Mary changed it and put a fresh, clean cloth on the table before setting it.

KEY VOCABULARY

VERBS
arrange
brush
hold
place
position
set
set down

NOUNS
ashtray
butter knife
china
crumb
dessert spoon
edge
fish fork
fish knife
flatware
goblet
napkin
serviette
shakers
side plate
silverware
soup spoon
table fork
table knife
tablecloth
tip
vase

OTHERS
bottom
centre
folded
fresh
in line with
left
middle
outer
right
soiled
under

FOR SPECIAL ATTENTION

- *setting the table* = arranging cutlery etc. on a table so that it is ready for use
- *set down* = put something in the correct place
- *china* [US] = another name for crockery [cups, plates etc.]
- *flatware* [US] = another name for cutlery. Also called *silverware* [US].
- *crumbs* = small bits of dry food
- *in line with...* = in a straight line with something
- *butter knife* = a short, blunt knife used to spread butter on bread
- *table knife and fork* = the knife and fork used when eating food other than fish or steak
- *fish knife and fork* = the special cutlery used for eating fish
- *steak knife* = a sharp knife with a serrated edge which cuts meat more easily
- *dessert spoon and fork* = the spoon and fork used for eating most desserts
- *soiled* = dirty or stained
- *oyster fork* = a small fork used for picking the oyster out of its shell
- *goblet* = a drinking glass with a stem and a base
- *napkin* = also called a *serviette* [UK]

Special Purpose Cutlery

- *oyster fork / steak knife* – these items are brought to the table only if the guest orders oysters or steak
- *fish knife and fork / soup spoon* – these items are removed from the place setting if the guests do **not** order fish or soup

Place Setting

NB: Some items in the place setting may be set in a slightly different position from the above description.

UNIT 15 – Exercises

1. **The items pictured below are used to set a table. Write down their names in the spaces provided.**

1. _____ 2. _____ 3. _____ 4. _____ 5. _____

6. _____ 7. _____ 8. _____ 9. _____ 10. _____

2. **Set this table for two! Draw the above items in their correct positions on the table below. Include side plates and butter knives.**

3. **Discuss with your trainer:**

   (a) the possible differences in position for some of the items in a place setting e.g. glasses

   (b) the shape and size of other special purpose flatware, e.g. fruit knife and fork, snail fork etc.

Checked Out Items 9/11/2019 15:16
XXXXXXXXXXXX6145

Item Title	Due Date
1. Main course : language and skills for restaurant workers 33305207090903	10/2/2019
2. 101 American customs : understanding American language and culture through common practices 33305203057216	10/2/2019
3. 5 little apples 33305239856658	10/2/2019
4. Spot, spike, spiral 33305245122993	10/2/2019

No of Items: 4

24/7 Telecirc: 800-471-0991
www.sccl.org
Thank you for visiting our library.

Santa Clara County Library District

408-293-2326

Checked Out Items 9/11/2019 15:16
XXXXXXXXXX6145

Item Title	Due Date
1. Main course : language and skills for restaurant workers 33305209270903	10/2/2019
2. 101 American customs : understanding American language and culture through common practices 33305230357216	10/2/2019
3. 5 little apples 33305239859659	10/2/2019
4. Spot, spike, spiral 33305245122993	10/2/2019

No of Items: 4

24/7 Telecirc: 800-471-0991
www.sccl.org
Thank you for visiting our library.

4. Use one of the words in the box to describe each <u>position</u> marked on the pictures below. Do not use the same word more than once.

right	in line with	top	outer	above
middle	under	centre	bottom	

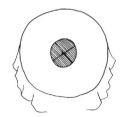

1. the _____ of the table

2. on the _____ of the guest

3. _____ the chair

4. the _____ edge of the table

5. the _____ side of the table knife

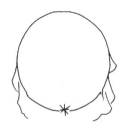

6. the _____ edge of the table

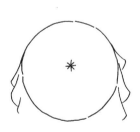

7. the _____ of the table

8. _____ the tip of the knife

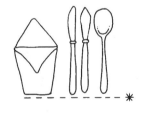

9. _____ the napkin

5. Match the words in column A with their meanings in column B.

A	B
1. soiled...........................[ ]	a. crockery
2. silverware...................[ ]	b. glass
3. china...........................[ ]	c. very small bits of food
4. goblet..........................[ ]	d. put into place
5. serviette.......................[ ]	e. the top end of something
6. crumbs.........................[ ]	f. stained or dirty
7. arrange........................[ ]	g. cutlery
8. tip................................[ ]	h. napkin

GLOSSARY

A collection of some useful words relating to food and service in restaurants. Users should note that the meanings given below are limited to the use of these words in a restaurant setting.

an à la carte menu [French] the restaurant's regular menu where each dish is charged individually at the price shown. Some restaurants may also have a special menu at a set price for lunch or for that day etc. Also **menu**. [p 22]

to address [someone] to use a particular name or title when speaking to someone. *She preferred to be addressed as Ms instead of Miss Jones.* [p 14]

an agreement acceptance of something. *She asked for the customer's agreement before changing his food order.* Also **to agree**. [p 47]

ahead in front of. *Walk ahead of the guests when you show them to their table.* [p 18]

to allow to give permission. *"Allow me." = "Let me do that for you."* [p 18]

an alternative another choice or option. *Offer the guest an alternative if the restaurant runs out of something that he orders.* [p 26]

angry not happy or pleased about something. [p 47]

to announce to call out the name of something. *The waiter announced each dish as he placed it in front of the guest.* [p 42]

to answer [the telephone] to pick up the receiver and speak to the caller. [p 14]

anti-clockwise in a direction opposite to the movements of the hands of a clock. [US] **counter clockwise**. [p 22]

an aperitif a drink [usually alcoholic] taken before meals. [p 22]

to apologize to say you are sorry. [p 46]

an apron a piece of clothing worn over the front part of the body to keep the wearer's clothes clean while working. [p 31]

to argue [with someone] to express an opposite opinion in an angry way. *Do not argue with customers if they complain about something.* [p 47]

to arrange to put things neatly and in order. *She arranged the dishes on the tray before taking them to the table.* [p 42]

an ashtray a small dish or container that smokers use for tobacco ash and cigarette butts. [p 31]

to assist to help, to do something for somebody. Also **assistance**. [p 14]

to attach to join a thing to something else. *First attach the filter to the machine, then press the start button.* [p 55]

to attend to take care of. *A waiter will attend to you shortly.* [p 18]

attention special care or action. Also **attentive, attentively**. [p 46]

available can be obtained. *Fresh salmon is available this month.* [p 26]

an aubergine [French] a dark purple vegetable. Also **brinjal**, [US] **eggplant**. See **Vegetables**. [p 11]

a bar a place or counter where alcoholic drinks are prepared and served. [p 46]

to barbecue to cook meat, fish etc. over an open fire. Also **broil, grill, charbroil**. [p 8]

a bartender [US] a person who serves and prepares drinks at the bar. Also **barman / barmaid**. [p 22]

a base the lowest part or bottom end of something. *Hold the glass by its base when you are placing it on the table.* [p 67]

a basin a round open bowl for holding liquids. [p 66]

behind in a position at the back of something. *The waiter kept his left arm behind his back as he worked.* [p 31]

a bill a written statement of the money owed for goods or services. *He paid the bill before he left the restaurant.* Also [US] **check**. [p 62]

a bin a large container for holding or storing things. [p 66]

bitter having a sharp flavour. *Black coffee tastes a little bitter.*

bland mild and having no definite flavour: *a bland cheese.* Opposites = **strong, spicy**.

blunt [knife] not sharp, does not cut easily. *A fish knife has a blunt edge.* Opposite = **sharp**. [p 30]

to boil to heat water or liquid to a high temperature until it begins to evaporate. Also **boiling**. *Tea is made with boiling water.* [p 8]

to book [a table] to reserve a table in advance. [p 14]

booked out [restaurant] the restaurant is full and cannot take any more customers. Also **fully booked, booked up**. [p 14]

bottom the lowest part of something. Opposite = **top**. [p 70]

a bowl a deep round dish used for holding food or liquid. [p 58]

a brandy a strong alcoholic drink made from grapes or other fruits. [p 59]

to break [something] to damage something so that it is no longer in one piece. *Be careful, those glasses break easily!* Also **broken**: *a broken dish*. [p 67]

to brew [tea or coffee] to add boiling water to coffee or tea and wait a few minutes for the mixture to reach its full flavour. Also **brewed** coffee / tea. [p 59]

bright shining or shiny *He polished the cutlery until it was bright and shiny.* Opposite = **dull**. [p 67]

to bring [something] to come carrying something. *Please bring me another cup of coffee.* Opposite = **take away**. [p 43]

to brush [something off] to remove something off a surface. *She brushed the crumbs off the table with a folded napkin.* [p 70]

a bucket a round open container, usually with handles, for liquid, ice etc. Also **ice-bucket, wine bucket**. [p 34]

a butt [cigarette] an end piece of a cigarette or cigar after it has been smoked. [p 31]

butter a creamy product made from milk, used in cooking or to spread on bread. [p 30]

a butter dish a small dish containing butter that is placed on the table. [p 30]

a butter knife a short blunt knife used to take butter from a dish. [p 71]

a button 1. a switch on a machine. [p 55] 2. a fastener on clothing. *The waiter fastened his collar button before going into the restaurant.*

a caller a person who makes a telephone call. [p 14]

a carafe a glass container for wine or water. [p 34]

carbonated [drink] containing bubbles of gas e.g. coca cola, soda-water, tonic etc. [p 12]

carefully with special attention. *Handle glassware carefully because it breaks easily.*

to carry to take something from one place to another. *The waitress carried the heavy tray of dishes to the kitchen.* [p 38]

a cart a table on wheels: *a dessert cart*. Also **trolley**. [p 54]

cash money in coins or notes. [p 63]

a cashier a person who receives and pays out money in a restaurant, shop etc. [p 62]

a cash register a machine used by the cashier in shops, restaurants etc.

a casserole food cooked in a covered heat-proof dish.

a celery a vegetable with long stems that can be eaten raw in salads or cooked. [p 11]

a centre [US **center**] the middle point or part of something: *the centre of the table*. [p 71]

a chair a seat with a back and sometimes with arms, for one person to sit on. [note: a **stool** has no back and arms] [p 18]

to change [something for something else] to replace one thing with another. *This glass is not clean, can you change it?* [p 48]

change 1. coins or notes equal to the value of a single note or coin. *Can you give me some change for a dollar?* 2. the money returned when the price of something is less than the money given in payment. *The customer got back some change after settling his bill with a $100 note.* [p 63]

char-broiled [steak etc.] cooked over an open fire. Also **barbecued, grilled, broiled**. [p 8]

to check to make sure of something by examining it. *She checked the food order before serving the guests.* [p 30]

a check [US] a bill. *The host asked the waiter for the check at the end of the meal.* [p 62]

a check-holder a folder that restaurants use to hold the check / bill when it is presented to the customer. [p 62]

a chef [French] the chief cook in a restaurant. [p 47]

cheese food made from milk: *a piece or slice of cheese*. Also **cheese cake, cheese board**.

china objects made of clay e.g. cups, saucers, plates etc. Also **crockery, dishes**. [p 7]

a chip a small piece that has broken off a glass or plate etc. A **chipped** glass = a glass that has a small piece broken off from its rim. [p 66]

clean washed, unused, free from dirt and stains. Opposite – **dirty, stained, used**. [p 66]

to clear [table] to take away dirty and used plates etc. after a meal. [p 50]

a clearing station an area in a restaurant to which dirty dishes are brought and left before they are washed up. Also **stewarding area**, [US] **bus station**. [p 51]

a cloakroom a small room where coats, hats, parcels etc. may be left for a time. [p 19]

clockwise move in the same direction as the hands of a clock. [p 22]

closed not open for business. *The restaurant is always closed on Mondays.*

a cloth a piece of material or fabric. Also cloth used for different purposes e.g. **washcloth, tablecloth, polishing cloth, dishcloth.** [p 67]

a coaster a small mat that is put under a drinking-glass. Also **glass-mat.** [p 22]

a cocktail an alcoholic drink made from spirits, or spirits mixed with fruit juice etc. See **Beverages – Alcoholic.** [p 13]

cold of low temperature. Opposite = **hot.** [p 30]

a cold kitchen a kitchen in a restaurant where salads and other cold dishes and desserts are prepared. Also [US] **cold line, cold side.** [p 30]

to collect to pick up or gather together. *Collect all the dirty dishes and take them to the kitchen.* [p 30]

to complain to find a fault, be dissatisfied with something. *The customer complained that his soup was too salty.* Also a **complaint.** *He told the manager about the guest's complaint.* [p 46]

to confirm to say something is true or correct. *The guests confirmed that the food order was correct.* Also **confirmation.** [p 27]

a contact number the telephone number of a person or company. [p 15]

to contain to have or hold inside itself. *The basket contained different kinds of bread.* Also **container.** [p 30]

to continue to go on doing something. *While the new customers studied the menu, she continued her work at another table.* [p 43]

a cork a type of bottle-stopper used especially for wine bottles. [p 34]

a corkscrew a tool used to pull corks out of bottles. Also **bottle-opener.** [p 34]

correct right or accurate. *The customer examined his bill to see if it was correct.* [p 38]

a course any of the separate parts of a meal, e.g. soup, dessert, main course etc. [p 38]

a cover 1. a lid that goes over something. *Food covers are put over the meals to keep the food warm.* 2. *A place setting. There are six covers on that table.* [p 23, 42]

to cover [for someone] to do another person's work. *The waiter had to serve more tables because he was covering for the sick waiter.*

a cover charge [in a restaurant] money to be paid in addition to the cost of food and drink.

a crack [in something] a line along which something has broken. Also **cracked:** *a cracked glass / plate* etc. [p 66]

cream thick, whitish liquid that is the fatty part of milk. Cream is used as an ingredient in many dishes, and is also eaten with many desserts: *whipped cream.* Also **creamy.**

a creamer [US] a small container for milk or cream which is put on the table. [Brit.] **milk jug.** [p 58]

a credit card a card that the owner uses instead of cash to pay for goods and services. [p 62]

crockery dishes made of clay or porcelain. Also **china, dishes, porcelain.** See also **Crockery.** [p 7]

a crumb a very small piece that has broken off food such as cake, bread, biscuits etc. *There were many crumbs on the table after the meal.* [p 70]

a customer a person who buys something in a shop or restaurant. Also a **guest** [in hotels and restaurants]. [p 18]

cutlery knives, spoons, and forks used for eating and serving food. Also [US] **silver or silverware, flatware.** [p 6]

a date 1. The specific day in the month and year, e.g. 23 May 2000 [p 14] 2. A sweet, brown fruit of a palm tree.

delicate [flavour] having a light, pleasant taste and texture: *a delicate wine / pastry* Opposites = **strong, full-bodied:** *a full-bodied wine.*

delicious having a very good taste or flavour.

a demitasse [French] a half-sized cup used in restaurants for espresso coffee. [p 55]

a desk a table or counter for the cashier / receptionist, in restaurants, hotels etc.: *reception desk.* Also **counter.** [p 19]

describe to say what something is like. *Waiters often have to describe a dish for their guests.* [p 26]

a dessert any sweet dish eaten at the end of a meal. Also [Brit.] **a sweet.** [p 54]

details small facts or item of information. [p 14]

to direct to show or tell someone the way to go. *The head-waiter directs guests to their tables.* Also **direction.** [p 18]

to discard to throw away something that is too old or broken. *Discard any glasses that are chipped or cracked.* [p 66]

a dish 1. a container for holding or serving food 2. A particular type of food prepared for a meal. *What are the main ingredients in this dish?* [p 26]

to dispense to give something out. *If you press that button the machine will dispense coffee into the cup.* [p 55]

to double-check to check a second time. *She double-checked the bill to make sure it was correct.* [p 38]

a dressing a sauce for food, especially salad. [p 43]

dry [wine] not sweet: *a dry white wine; a dry sherry.*

dull [cutlery] not bright and shining. [p 67]

empty having nothing inside. *She poured wine into the empty glasses.* Opposite = **full**. [p 31]

an entrée [Brit] food served before the main course. Also **starter, appetizer, first course**. [p 27]

an entrée [US] the main course. [p 27]

equal the same in size, shape and amount. *Cut the cake into ten equal slices.*

equipment the things needed for a particular purpose. *The equipment for mixing drinks is kept at the bar.* [p 55]

etiquette the rules of correct and polite behaviour. *It is good restaurant etiquette to thank each guest when they leave the restaurant.* [p 31]

to examine [something] to look carefully at something. *Examine each glass for chips or cracks before putting it on the table.* [p 62]

to explain to make something more clear to somebody. *The waiter explained why the restaurant had to close early.* Also an **explanation**. [p 26]

extra more than what is usual. *The customers asked for extra bread and butter.* [p 23]

eye-contact [with somebody] looking directly into the eyes of somebody. *Make eye-contact with the guest when you speak to him.* [p 19]

face-down [cups or glassware] upside down. *Glasses are placed face-down on the tray to keep them free from dust.* [p 66]

fat an oily substance from plants or animals that is used for cooking, e.g. frying, roasting etc. Oil, butter, and margarine are all fats.

to fill [something] to put liquids or solids into something. *Fill the sugar bowl and take it to the table.* [p 58]

to filter to separate unwanted solid material from a liquid e.g. coffee. Also a **filter**. [p 55]

finally lastly, or at the end. [p 71]

to finish to reach the end of a task or activity. *When you finish polishing the cutlery, you can set the table.* Opposite = **to start**.

a first course the first dish served and eaten at a meal. Also **starter**, [British] **entrée, appetizer**. [p 38]

a fish knife a blunt knife with a broad blade used for eating fish. See **Cutlery**. [p 6]

flatware [US] cutlery. [p 6]

flavour [US **flavor**] the taste and smell of food. *Ingredients like garlic and herbs add flavour to food.* Also to **flavour, flavoured**: *a sauce flavoured with lemon.* [p 26]

a food order form a written record of all the food items that are ordered by guests. Also **food pad**. [p 26]

a floor-chart an outline drawing of the position of all the tables in the restaurant. Also **floor-plan, seating chart**. [p 19]

a foil a very thin, flexible, metallic sheet used for wrapping food. [p 34]

to fold to turn something so that one part of it lies on another. *The table napkin is folded into a triangular shape and placed on the guest's lap.* [p 18]

a forearm the part of the arm from the elbow to the fingertips. *He carried the tray of beverages on his forearm.*

fresh [food] 1. food that is not frozen, preserved, or canned. 2. Newly made or produced. [p 26]

froth a mass of small bubbles on the surface of a liquid. Also **foam**. [p 55]

to froth [up] to cause a liquid to produce froth. *Milk is frothed up by steam, then poured into a cup of coffee.* [p 55]

to garnish to decorate or make food look attractive, usually with small pieces of fruit or vegetables like parsley, lemon etc.

gin a colourless, alcoholic drink, flavoured with juniper berries. See **Beverages – Alcoholic**. [p 13]

glassware all the different glasses in a bar or restaurant. [p 6, 66]

to go through [something] to study or check something carefully. *Go through the bill and make sure it is correct.* [p 62]

a goblet a drinking glass which has a stem and base, but no handle. [p 71]

greasy [food] containing too much oil or fat.

to greet to say words like 'Good morning / Welcome' etc. when meeting or receiving a guest. Also a **greeting**. [p 18]

to grind to crush something e.g. pepper, coffee etc. into powder or very small pieces. [p 43]

a grinder the equipment, either mechanical or electrical, that grinds something: *a coffee-grinder*. [p 55]

to grip to hold something firmly so that it does not move or fall. *He gripped the cutlery on the plate as he lifted it off the table.* [p 50]

ground [food] food that has been reduced to a powder or very small pieces, e.g. coffee, pepper, meat. [p 43]

half [pic] a specific quantity: *half a glass* = see also **one-third, three-quarters**. [p 35]

a handle [cutlery, crockery] the part of a spoon, cup etc by which it may be held. [p 42]

a head-waiter the person who supervises the work and the staff of a restaurant. [p 14]

heavy 1. [food] rich and difficult to digest: a heavy meal. 2. [objects] weighing a lot. Opposite = **light**.

a herb a plant whose leaves or seeds are used to flavour food. Also **herbal** [tea]. [p 11]

a host the person who invites others as guests, to a meal, party etc. [US] A host can also be the person who takes reservations, greets guests, and shows guests to the table in a restaurant. Also **hostess** [female], to **host**. [p 38, 39]

hot [food] 1. having a high temperature because of being heated. *The coffee was too hot to drink.* 2. producing a burning sensation to taste because of the spices used e.g. chilli, pepper, mustard etc. *Sri Lankan curries are usually very hot.*

a hot kitchen a kitchen in a restaurant where the hot dishes are prepared. Also [US] **hot line, hot side**. [p 30]

a house wine a wine that is specially selected and sold a little more cheaply in the restaurant. [p 34]

an ice cream a sweet, frozen food made from cream and flavoured with fruits etc. [p 54]

an index finger the finger next to the thumb. [p 42]

to indicate [something to somebody] to show what you want or mean by pointing or some other sign. *The guest indicated that he wanted his check by raising his hand.* [p 39]

to inform to tell someone something. *The waiter informed the manager about the guest's complaint.* Also **information**. [p 46]

an ingredient any of the foods that are used to make a particular dish. [p 26]

to insist [on something] demand something and not accept refusal for an answer. *The difficult guest insisted on a table although the restaurant was booked out.* [p 46]

an instant coffee a processed coffee powder that does not need to be brewed. The coffee is made by simply pouring hot water over the coffee powder and stirring to mix.

instead as an alternative or replacement. *We have no more salmon. Would you like to try the trout instead?*

to interrupt [somebody] to stop somebody speaking by doing or saying something. *Don't interrupt the guests without excusing yourself first.* [p 26]

to introduce [oneself] to give your name and say who you are. *The waiter introduced himself to the guests and gave them the menu.* [p 22]

a jug a container with a handle for holding and pouring liquids: *water / milk jug.* [US] **pitcher**. [p 55, 58]

a juice liquid from fruit or vegetables. Also **juicy** = containing liquid or juice.

to justify to say that something is right or correct. *If a guest complains about your mistake, do not try to justify yourself.* [p 47]

to keep an eye on [something] to watch and make sure something is all right. *The service is good in that restaurant because the head-waiter keeps an eye on all the workers.* [p 43]

a kitchen a place where meals are cooked or prepared. [p 30]

a label a piece of paper on a bottle or can that describes its contents. *The wine label tells where and when the wine was made.* [p 34]

a lap the upper part of a seated person's thighs. *The waitress folded a napkin and placed it on the guest's lap.* [p 18]

to lay a table to put cutlery, glasses etc. in their correct positions on a table in readiness for a meal. Also to **set a table**. [p 70]

largest the biggest in size. *He stacked the dishes with the largest plates at the bottom.* [p 51]

to leave to go away from a place or person. *They left the restaurant when it closed at midnight.* [p 63]

light [something] to start something burning. *She took a lighter out of her pocket and lit the guest's cigarette.* [p 31]

light [food] food that is small in quantity, does not contain rich ingredients, and is easy to digest. *A salad is a light meal.* [p 26]

lined [tray] a tray which has a cloth or napkin on it. *Place the clean glasses on a lined tray.* [p 66]

linen items made of cloth: *table-cloths, napkins etc.*

lint tiny dust-like bits of fabric that cloth sometimes leaves on a glass surface. [p 66]

a lipstick stain a mark or stain on a glass or cup made when someone wearing lipstick drinks from it. [p 66]

a liqueur a strong, sweet, alcoholic spirit drunk in small quantities especially after a meal. See also **Beverages – Alcoholic**. [p 13]

a lunch a meal eaten in the middle of the day.

a main course the most important or biggest part of a meal. [US] **entrée**. [p 42]

to make a reservation [restaurant] to ask for a table in advance of a certain date. Also to **reserve, to book**. [p 14]

a meal food that is served or eaten. *He enjoyed his meal at that restaurant.* [p 38]

medium [for meat] meat that is not cooked too long or too little. See also **rare, well-done**. [p 26]

mellow [wine] having a soft, ripe flavour or taste: *a*

mellow red wine. Opposites = **sharp, dry, young.**

a menu a list of the dishes available at a restaurant. [p 22]

moist not dry, slightly wet. *Try the chocolate cake. It's rich and moist.* Also to **moisten.**

mousse a sweet or savoury dish made from cream and eggs, and flavoured with other ingredients.

mustard a sharp-flavoured, yellow spice used in cooking, or often served with meat dishes.

a napkin a piece of cloth or paper used at meals to protect clothes and wipe one's lips and fingers. [Brit] **serviette.** [p 18]

non-smoking [place] an area in a restaurant or public place where smoking is not allowed. [p 14]

a nozzle end-piece of a pipe through which air, steam, or liquid can be directed e.g. the steam nozzle on a coffee machine. [p 55]

to offer [something] to give something, or ask if you can do something for somebody. *He offered them coffee and liqueurs after their meal. The head-waiter offered to get them a taxi.* [p 43]

on the house no payment required: *the drinks are on the house* = the restaurant will not charge for the drinks.

to order to ask a waiter for food or drink items on the menu. Also an **order.** [p 26]

an oven a box-like piece of kitchen equipment for cooking or heating food. See **Cooking Methods.** [p 8]

over-cooked cooked too much. Opposite = **undercooked.** [p 46]

an oyster a type of shellfish, usually eaten uncooked. See also **Seafood.** [p 9]

a packet a small paper container: *a packet of sugar.* Also **sachet, bag.**

a palm the inner surface of the hand. [p 42]

a pantry a small space or room in some restaurants where food items or food-related equipment are kept. [p 55]

parsley a small-leafed green herb, used in cooking or to garnish a dish. See **Vegetables.** [p 11]

a party 1. a group of people. *His reservation was for a party of eight.* 2. A social occasion to which people are invited. *She booked the whole restaurant for her birthday party.* [p 14]

pasta food made from flour, eggs, and water and cut into various shapes e.g. macaroni, ravioli, spaghetti etc.

a pastry a mixture of flour, fat and water baked in an oven and used as a base or covering for tarts, pies etc.

to pay to give money for goods or services. Also **payment:** *a cash payment.* [p 63]

a pepper mill a container in which pepper is ground to a powder. [p 43]

to perform to do or carry out a task. *She kept an eye on the tables as she performed her tasks in the restaurant.*

to pick [up] to collect. *She picked up the meals for table 6 as soon as they were ready in the kitchen.* [p 42]

to pierce to make a hole with a sharp pointed instrument. *First pierce the wine-bottle cork with the opener, then turn the opener clockwise into the cork.* [p 34]

to place to put something down in a particular place. *She placed the teapot next to the cup.* Also a **place.** [p 22]

a place-mat a mat on a table on which a person's plates and cutlery are put. Also **tablemat.** [p 23]

a place-setting a set of cutlery, dishes etc. on a table, for one person. Also **cover.** [p 23]

a plate a flat, dish from which food is served or eaten. See **Crockery.** [p 7]

a pocket an additional piece of material on some clothing [e.g. coat, apron, jacket etc.] for carrying things in. *A waitress often carries a pen in her apron pocket.* [p 31]

to polish to rub something until it becomes clean and shiny. [p 66]

a portion a quantity of food served to one person. *She gave him a large portion of cake.* [p 42]

a position a place for something. *The correct position for the side-plate is on the left of the place setting.* [p 71]

to prepare to get or make something ready. *After lunch they prepared the tables for dinner.* [p 47]

to present to give something formally to somebody. *The check is put into a check-holder and presented to the customer.* [p 62]

to press to push. *When you press this button, the machine will start making coffee.* [p 55]

to process [a credit card] to make certain checks on the use of the card. [p 62]

quarter one of four equal parts of something. [p 35]

a rack of lamb a popular lamb dish made with ribs.

rare [meat] meat e.g. steak or a roast that is lightly cooked and still pink in colour. See also **well-done, medium.** [p 26]

raw not cooked or uncooked.

ready fully prepared. *Are you ready to order now?* [p 38]

a receipt a written statement that money has been paid for something. Also **payment voucher.** [p 63]

to recommend to tell a customer about a dish or food that you think is good. *I recommend the pasta dishes, they are the chef's speciality.* Also a **recommendation**. [p 26]

to record to write down information for later use. *The waiter must record all the drinks that are ordered on an order form.* Also a **record**. [p 15]

to refill to fill again, an empty glass, cup etc. [p 39]

to remove to take something away from somewhere. *She removed the dirty dishes from the table and took them to the kitchen.* [p 51]

to repeat to say something more than once. *After they had ordered their food, the waiter repeated their order back to them.* [p 22]

to replace 1. to put something back in its place. 2. provide a substitute for something. *She replaced the table knife with a steak knife.* [p 30]

to request to ask for something. Also a **request**. [p 14]

to reserve to keep or hold a table for someone's use at a later date or time. Also to **book**. [p 14]

a reservation a table that has been kept or held for someone. Also **booking**. [p 14]

a rib cut of meat from the chest portion of an animal. See **Meat**. [p 10]

rich [food] containing a large amount of fat, butter, cream etc.: *a rich sauce / cake / casserole etc.*

a rim the top or outer edge of a glass, cup, plate etc. *Make sure there are no chips on the rims of the glasses.* [p 66]

a roll [bread] a piece of bread that has a rounded shape. [p 30]

to roast to cook food in an oven. See **Cooking Methods**. [p 8] Also a **roast**.

rosemary a herb whose leaves are used to flavour food. See **Vegetables**. [p 11]

a sachet a small sealed bag or packet containing a product like sugar, salt, sauce etc. Also **packet, bag**. [p 58]

saccharin a sweet substance used in place of sugar.

sage a herb used to flavour food: *a sage and onion stuffing.* See **Vegetables**. [p 11]

a salad a dish of raw vegetables like lettuce, cucumber, tomatoes etc. often seasoned with a dressing. [p 11, 17]

a salmon a large fish with pinkish flesh. **Smoked salmon** is salmon that has been preserved or cured with smoke, then sliced thinly and served cold. See **Seafood**. [p 9]

satisfied feeling pleased. *Customers are usually satisfied with the meals and service in a good restaurant.* [p 46]

a sauce a thick liquid served with food to add flavour. [p 43]

a saucepan a cooking pot with a lid and a handle, used for cooking things over heat.

a saucer a small dish on which a cup is placed. See also **Crockery**. [p 7]

to sauté French term for frying food in a little oil or fat. See **Cooking Methods**. [p 8]

savoury [US **savory**] food having a salty or sharp flavour: *a savoury pancake.* Opposite = **sweet**.

a scoop a sort of spoon used for serving food e.g. ice-cream. Also to **scoop** – to pick up a certain amount of food with a spoon or scoop. [p 42]

to scrape to use something e.g. a fork, to remove food from a dish. [p 50]

to season to flavour food with salt, pepper, herbs etc.: *seasoned with lemon and garlic.*

a section part of a room or restaurant: *the smoking / non-smoking sections of a restaurant.*

to select to choose from a list, menu etc. *He selected an Australian red wine from the wine list.* Also a **selection**. [p 34]

to serve to give food etc. to guests and attend to their needs at a table. Also **service, server, serving spoon / fork.**

a serviette a cloth or paper used while eating to protect one's clothes or wipe one's fingers or lips: [US] **napkin**. [p 18]

a set a group of similar things: *cutlery, crockery, a tea set.* Also a **place setting** or **setting**. [p 23]

to set [a table] to place in position all the cutlery and crockery needed for a meal. [p 23, 70]

shakers containers for pepper and salt. Also a **cocktail shaker** = a container for mixing drinks. [p 71]

sharp 1. as in a knife edge that cuts meat etc. easily. Opposite = **blunt**. [p 30] 2. [food] having a strong or definite flavour, e.g. certain cheeses, lemon, mustard.

a sherry a fortified wine usually drunk as an aperitif. See also **Alcoholic Drinks**. [p 13, 22]

a side plate a small plate placed on the left side of a place setting. Also **bread plate**. [p 71]

to sign to write one's name on a document. [p 62]

a signature a person's name written by that person. [p 63]

silverware 1. cutlery made of metal. Also **flatware** 2. Dishes, cutlery, and other items made of silver. [p 6]

single one only: *a single scoop of ice-cream.*

a sitting a period of time when a group of people eat a meal. *The restaurant has two sittings for dinner – one early in the evening, and the other from about 9pm onwards.*

a slice a thin flat piece cut off an item of food: *a slice of cake, bread, meat, cheese etc.* [p 30]

smoking in a restaurant, refers to the area or section where guests may smoke cigarettes etc.: *a table in smoking.* Also **non-smoking**. [p 14]

a smudge a dirty mark. [p 67]

a snifter a glass shaped like a small bowl on a stem: *a brandy snifter.* See **Glassware**. [p 6]

a soda [US] any carbonated [i.e. fizzy with gas bubbles] soft drink. [p 12]

a soda [water] a carbonated drink often used as a mixer for spirits e.g. whiskey. [p 12]

a soft drink any cold, non-alcoholic beverage. [p 12]

soiled dirty: *a soiled tablecloth.* [p 71]

a sole a flat sea-fish. See **Seafood**. [p 9]

a sorbet a water-ice made from water, sugar and fruit or vegetable juice. Sorbets are often served between courses.

a soup a liquid food made by cooking meat, vegetables etc, in water. Also **soup-bowl, soup-spoon**.

sour 1. having a sharp taste, like vinegar or lemons. 2. not fresh: *sour milk* 3. fermented: *sour cream.* Also to **turn sour** = to taste bad or unpleasant.

spaghetti pasta made in long thin rods.

sparkling [wine or water] containing tiny bubbles of gas: *a sparkling white wine.* Opposite = **still**.

sparkling very bright and shiny. *The crystal glasses were spotless and sparkling.* [p 66]

a speciality [US **specialty**] a dish or food for which a restaurant is well-known. *Char-broiled steak is the speciality of that restaurant.* [p 54]

special purpose cutlery knives, forks etc. used for a specific purpose: *a fruit knife, an oyster fork, a grapefruit spoon.* [p 71]

spices plants with strong taste and smell, used usually in a dried and powdered form, to flavour food: *ginger, nutmeg, cinnamon, pepper etc. are all spices.* Also to **spice, spicy, spiced**.

to spill to accidentally cause liquid to fall out of its container. *The guest knocked over a glass and spilt the wine all over the tablecloth.*

a spirit a strong distilled alcoholic drink: *brandy, rum, gin, whiskey etc.* [p 13]

a spoon a piece of cutlery. See **Cutlery**. [p 6] Also **soup-spoon, dessert-spoon, teaspoon, tablespoon**.

spotless very clean with no stains or marks: *a spotless tablecloth.* [p 66]

a spout the part of something e.g. a teapot, from or through which liquid pours out. [p 55]

to sprinkle to throw something in small drops or bits onto a surface. *She sprinkled chocolate powder over the cappuccino.* [p 55]

to stack to put one thing on top of another. *He stacked the dirty dishes on a tray and took them to the kitchen.* [p 51]

a stain a dirty mark or patch of colour. *It is difficult to clean a red wine stain on a tablecloth.* [p 66]

stale [food] not fresh and tasting unpleasant: *stale bread, biscuits, cake etc.* Opposite = **fresh**.

a stand a small piece of furniture on which something may be placed: *a tray-stand, a wine-bucket stand.* [p 34, 38]

a starter the first course of a meal. Also [US] **appetizer**. [p 26]

a steak a thick piece of meat or fish cut for frying or grilling. See also **Meat**. [p 26]

to steam to cook food over boiling water. See **Cooking Methods**. [p 8]

a stem 1. part of a glass. [p 67]
2. part of a leafy vegetable.

to stew to cook something in liquid in a closed pan. See **Cooking Methods**. [p 8] Also a **stew**.

a steward person who does work at the back of a restaurant e.g clearing or washing up dishes etc. [US] **busboy, busperson**. [p 51]

a stewarding area place in a restaurant where used dishes etc. are collected before being washed up. Also **clearing station**, [US] **bus station**. [p 51]

to stir to mix something in a container using a spoon etc.

a stirrer a thin plastic stick used to mix a drink in a glass. Also **swizzle-stick**. [p 22]

strong [drink] 1. Highly flavoured: *a strong coffee.* 2. containing more of something e.g. alcohol. *Pour me a strong whisky.* Opposites = **bland, mild, tasteless**. [p 55]

a stock liquid made by stewing meat, fish etc. in water, used as a base for soups, sauces etc.

to stuff to put something e.g. chopped onions, mushrooms etc., into something e.g. a turkey, fish or chicken before cooking it. Also a **stuffing**.

to suggest to tell a guest about a dish he may like to order. *The waiter suggested that they try the fresh lobster.* Also to **recommend**. [p 54]

a supper a late night meal, usually less food than at dinner.

sweet tasting like sugar. Opposites = **sour, bitter, salty**. Also Brit. **a sweet** = a dessert.

a sweetener a chemical substance used instead of sugar to sweeten drinks or food. [p 58]

a table fork the fork used to eat the main course of a meal. See **Cutlery**. [p 6] Also **dinner fork, joint fork.**

a table knife the knife used to eat the main course of a meal. See **Cutlery**. [p 6] Also **dinner knife, joint knife.**

a tablecloth the cloth used to cover a table. See **Equipment – Other**. [p 7]

to take [a reservation / food order] to write down the details of a reservation or food order. [p 14]

tart sharp or sour-tasting, like lemons or vinegar. Also **a tart** = pastry containing fruit or other sweet filling. [p 54]

to taste to try a small quantity of food or drink. *The customer always tastes the wine before it is served.* [p 35]

tasty having a pleasant flavour, good to eat or drink: *a tasty dish.* Opposites = **tasteless, bland.**

a tea a hot or cold beverage made from the leaves of the tea plant or other herbal plants e.g. camomile, mint etc. [p 58]

a tea-bag a small paper packet containing enough tea for one cup. Also **tea-leaf** [pl – leaves], **teapot, teacup, teaspoon.** [p 58]

tender [meat] soft and easy to chew. Opposite = **tough**. [p 49]

three-quarter a specific quantity in a container. *Do not fill a cup or glass more than three-quarter full with any beverage.* [p 58]

thyme a herb.

a tip a small sum of money given by a customer to a waiter for his good service. [p 62]

a title a word used to show a person's status, rank, or occupation: *Queen, Major, Doctor, Sir, Lord, Mrs. etc.* [p 14]

tongs [a pair of tongs] an instrument used for picking up things e.g. sugar cubes, ice.

a tonic [water] a carbonated drink often used as a mixer with spirits: *a gin tonic.* [p 12 , 22]

to top up to fill a partly empty glass or cup. *He topped up the wine glasses.* Also **fill up, refill.** [p 31]

a tossed salad a salad that has been mixed with a dressing e.g. oil and vinegar.

tough [meat] hard to cut or chew: *a tough steak.* [p 49]

a tray-stand a piece of furniture on which a tray can be placed. [p 38]

triangular in the shape of a triangle. ▲ *Napkins are folded*

into a triangular shape before being placed on a guest's lap. [p 18]

a trolley a table on wheels used for displaying or serving food: *a dessert trolley.* Also **cart.** [p 54]

a trout a freshwater fish. See **Seafood**. [p 9]

a truffle 1. a type of expensive mushroom with a rich flavour. 2. a sweet or dessert made from chocolate.

a tumbler a drinking glass with no handle or stem.

a tuna a large sea-fish.

a turkey a large bird eaten especially at Christmas: *a slice of roast turkey.* See **Poultry**. [p 9]

to upset to make somebody angry or unhappy. *The rude waiter upset the customer.* [p 47]

unused new or clean: *an unused tablecloth / plate etc.* Opposites = **dirty, old.** [p 23]

a vase a container for holding cut flowers. [p 71]

a vegetable the part of a plant, its root, stem or leaves, that is eaten as food. [p 11]

to verify to make sure that something is true or accurate. *She verified the customer's signature by looking at his credit card.* [p 63]

a vinaigrette [French] a mixture of oil, vinegar and herbs, used as a salad dressing.

vinegar a sour liquid used for flavouring or preserving food, and in salad dressings. [p 43]

a vineyard a place where grapes are grown, especially for making wine.

vintage [wine] 1. the wine made from the grapes harvested in a specific season and area. *The 1961 Bordeaux wines were a great vintage.* 2. [adj] excellent, outstanding, of high quality. *This is a vintage Bordeaux.*

a vol-au-vent [French] a small light case of puff pastry filled with meat, fish etc.

a voucher a document or receipt showing that money has been paid for goods. Also **receipt**. [p 63]

a waiter a person employed to take customers' orders, bring food etc. in a restaurant. Female = **waitress**. Also **a server**. [p 22]

a waiter's station an area in a restaurant where some dishes, salt and pepper shakers, ashtrays etc. are kept. Also **wait station**. [p 30]

to warm [up] something to make something hot. *I'm sorry your food is cold, I'll warm it up for you.*

a water spot a small mark that water sometimes leaves when it dries on glass. [p 66]

well-done [meat] cooked for a longer time or until meat is no longer pink. [p 26]

a whisky [US **whiskey**] a strong alcoholic drink made from grain especially barley or rye. [p 13]

wholemeal [bread etc] made from a light-brown flour that contains the whole grain of wheat, i.e. the husk etc. [US] **whole wheat**. [p 30]

wine alcoholic drink made from the juice of grapes or other fruits. See **Beverages – Alcoholic**. [p 34]

a wine list a printed list of the wines available in a restaurant. [p 34]

yoghurt a thick, slightly sour milk product. Also **yogurt**.

ANSWER KEY

UNIT 1

1. waiter   reservation record   date   non-smoking sign
   notepad   floor chart   caller   window table
2. time   number   name   contact number
   smoking or non-smoking   special requests
3. 1. [e]   2. [f]   3. [g]   4. [h]
   5. [b]   6. [c]   7. [d]   8. [a]
4. six thirty or half past six   nine o'clock or nine [a.m./p.m.]
   a quarter to seven or six forty-five
   twenty past eight or eight twenty
5. the twenty-third of May / May twenty-third
   the twelfth of December / December twelfth
   the second of June / June second
   the thirty-first of December / December thirty-first
6. 1. [c]   2. [d]   3. [a]   4. [b]
   5. [g]   6. [h]   7. [e]   8. [f]
7. 1. For which date?   2. Just a moment, please, I'll see if we
   have one.   3. For what time?
   4. Could you give me a contact number, please?

UNIT 2

1. 1. showing   2. pulling out   3. seating
   4. picking up   5. folding   6. welcoming
2. 1. chair   2. triangle   3. pace   4. details
   5. palm   6. party   7. napkin   8. lap
3. 1. ahead   2. satisfied   3. clearly
   4. shortly   5. made eye-contact with   6. nearest
4. a. 4   b. 1   c.2   d. 3
5. See DIALOGUES Unit 2 Ex. 5 page 86.

UNIT 3

1. 1. a food order   2. cutlery / flatware   3. beverages
   4. a place setting   5. crockery / china   6. aperitifs
2. 1. clockwise   2. take away   3. correct
   4. picked up   5. unused   6. empty
3. 1. coaster   2. bartender   3. menu   4. tray
   5. waiter's station   6. placemat   7. waitress   8. stirrer
4. 1. [f]   2. [e]   3. [d]   4. [a]   5. [c]   6. [b]
5. See DIALOGUES Unit 3 Ex. 5 page 86.

UNIT 4

1. [a] 4   [b] 2   [c] 8   [d] 7
   [e] 1   [f] 5   [g] 3   [h] 6
2. 1. meal   2. dish   3. specialities   4. alternative
   5. starter 6. ingredients 7. main course 8. for confirmation
3. 1. [c]   2. [d]   3. [a]   4. [e]   5. [b]
4. [b] 8   [c] 2   [d] 1   [e] 6   [f] 7   [g] 3   [h] 5
5. Correct order: 1. h   2. d   3. a   4. e 5. c   6. b 7. f 8. g
   See DIALOGUES Unit 4 Ex. 5 page 86.

UNIT 5

1 (A) 1. collecting   2. replacing   3. topping up   4. lifting
   5. removing   6. placing   7. preparing
   8. reaching across   9. lighting   10. bringing
(B) 1. He is collecting glasses from the waiter's station.
   2. She is replacing the knife with a steak knife.
   3. She is topping up a glass of wine.
   4. He is lifting the used ashtray off the table.
   5. She is removing the unused place setting.
   6. He is placing a bread basket on the table.
   7. The chef is preparing a meal.
   8. She is lighting the guest's cigarette.
   9. He is bringing a water jug to the table.
2. right / left   sharp / blunt   full / empty   clean / used
   over / under   cold / hot   rounded / flat
   behind / in front of

3. 1. kitchen   2. apron   3. butter   4. pocket   5. jug
   6. lighter   7. butt   8. wholemeal   9. ashtray   10. slice

UNIT 6

1 (A) a. remove   b. pierce   c. unscrew   d. turn clockwise
   e. cut   f. wipe   g. show   h. press down
   (B) 1. g   2. e   3. a   4. f   5. b   6. d   7. h   8. c
2. (A) bowl   (B) label, cork   (C) top
3. 1. bulge   2. foil wrapper.   3. label   4. cork
   5. neck   6. base
4. 1. stand   2. below   3. cork   4. label   5. taste
   6. set up   7. pull out 8. fill   9. show   10. wipe

UNIT 7

1. [a] up   [b] down   [c] out of   [d] away
   [e] with   [f] out   [g] up   [h] from
2. 1. host / hostess   2. double-checked   3. announced
   4. indicated   5. topped up
3. 1. head   2. shoulder   3. palm   4. arm
   5. hand   6. fingers   7. knee
4. 1. b 2. e   3. a 4. c   5. d
5. 1. label   2. coaster   3. bartender   4. ingredient
   5. cork   6. recommend   7. cutlery   8. reservation
   9. beverages   10. entrée   11. aperitif   12. stirrer

UNIT 8

1. 1. the main course   2. freshly ground pepper   3. sauce
   4. salad dressing   5. vegetables   6. bread
2. (A) [a] checked   [b] carried   [c] took off   [d] announced
   [e] put   [f] arranged   [g] set   [h] collected
   [i] offered   [j] placed   [k] wished
   (B) 1. h   2. a   3. f   4. e   5. b   6. g
   7. j   8. c   9. d   10. i   11. k
3. 1. thumb; index   2. pepper mill   3. covers
   4. main portion   5. tray stand   6. serving spoon and fork
   7. handle   8. vinegar
4. 2; 3; 6

UNIT 9

1. (a) 2   (b) 6   (c) 1   (d) 3   (e) 5   (f) 4
2. 1. (a)   2. (c)   3. (d)   4. (b)   5. (e)   6. (f)
3. (A) Dialogue 1: 1. T   2. F   3. F   4. F   5. T
   Dialogue 2: 1. F   2. F   3. F   4. T   5. T
   (B) See DIALOGUES Unit 9 Ex. 3(B) page 86.

Unit 10

1. firstly / finally   top / bottom   heaviest / lightest
   over / under   dirty / unused   smallest / largest
   leave / arrive   satisfied / upset
2. 1. cleared   2. heaviest   3. Grip   4. scrape
   5. stacked   6. study   7. clearing station
   8. finally   9. largest   10. transferred
3. 1. flowers or vase of flowers   2. slices of bread
   3. bread rolls   4. bread basket
   5. salt and pepper shakers   6. butter dish   7. ash tray
4. 1. d   2. c   3. a   4. g   5. f   6. k
   7. l   8. b   9. j   10. h   11. e   12. i

Unit 11

1. 1. trolley / cart   2. froth   3. cake   4. pantry
   5. jug / pitcher   6. demitasse   7. steam   8. tart
2. 1. dispensing   2. sprinkling   3. attaching   4. pressing
   5. frothing up   6. pouring
3. 1. coffee machine   2. steam nozzle   3. button
   4. coffee beans   5. ground coffee   6. coffee grinder
   7. spout   8. filter

4. 1. (c)   2. (a)   3. (b)   4. (c)   5. (a)   6. (d)
    5. See DIALOGUES Unit 11 Ex. 5 page 86.

Unit 12
1. 1. teapot   2. an espresso coffee   3. a cappuccino
    4. teacup   5. teaspoon   6. saucer
    7. milk jug (creamer)   8. sugar bowl
2. 1. warm   2. putting   3. teapot   4. pour out
    5. teabag   6. tea-leaves   7. three-quarters
    8. boiling   9. brew   10. teacup   11. sugar
3. 1. [c]   2. [e]   3. [g]   4. [h]
    5. [b]   6. [d]   7. [a]   8. [f]
4. 1. a soft drink / glass of coke   2. a glass of red wine
    3. a brandy   4. a liqueur   5. a glass of white wine
    6. a beer
5. See DIALOGUES Unit 12 Ex. 5 page 86.

Unit 13
1. 1. credit card   2. cash   3. signature   4. check / bill
    5. cashier   6. check holder
2. (a) examined   (b) included   (c) signed   (d) verified
    (e) processed   (f) asked   (g) gave   (h) took
3. 1. (f)   2. (a)   3. (g)   4. (h)
    5. (e)   6. (b)   7. (c)   8. (d)
4. 1. T   2. F   3. F   4. T
    5. T   6. T   7. T   8. F
5. 1. E   2. B   3. C   4. D   5. A
6. See DIALOGUES Unit 13 Ex. 5 [b] page 87.

Unit 14
1. stained   broken   dirty   cracked
    chipped   smudged
2. 1. stained   2. cracked   3. smudged   4. broken
    5. chipped   6. dirty
3. 1. spotless   2. bright   3. polished   4. shiny
    5. sparkling
4. 1. inserted   2. overlapped   3. rotate   4. lined
    5. face down   6. noticed
5. 1. lipstick stain   2. washed   3. water-spots   4. lint
    5. hold   6. basin   7. steam   8. moistened
    9. polish   10. chip   11. rim   12. discard bin
    13. dull   14. polishing   15. handle   16. fingerprint
    17. smudges   14. base   15. face down   16. between

Unit 15
1. 1. napkin / serviette   2. table knife and fork   3. ashtray
    4. water glass / goblet   5. salt and pepper shakers
    6. fish knife and fork   7. wine glass   8. dessert fork
    and spoon   9. vase of flowers   10. soup spoon
2. See Unit 15 page 71, picture frames 15 – 19
4. 1. middle   2. right   3. under   4. top   5. outer
    6. bottom   7. centre   8. above   9. in line with
5. 1. [f]   2. [g]   3. [a]   4. [b]
    5. [h]   6. [c]   7. [d]   8. [e]

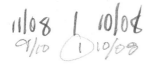

DIALOGUES

(Dialogues in Exercise pages)

UNIT 2 Exercise 5 [page 21]
Waiter: Good evening. Welcome to Chez Max.
Guest: Good evening. A table for two, please.
Waiter: Do you have a reservation, madam?
Guest: No, we don't.
Waiter: Would you like smoking or non-smoking?
Guest: Non-smoking, please.
Waiter: Yes, we have a table for you. Would you mind waiting a few minutes? We'll get it ready for you now.
Guest: Yes, that's fine. We'll wait over there.
Waiter: Could I take your coats?
Guests: Oh yes, thank you.
Waiter: Your table is ready, madam. Could you follow me please?

UNIT 3 Exercise 5 [page 25]
Waiter: Good evening. My name's Dave. I'll be serving your table.
Guest: Good evening.
Waiter: This is our á la carte menu.
Guest: Thank you.
Waiter: Would you like to order an aperitif?
Guest: Yes. A dry sherry, please.
Waiter: Certainly, madam.
And for you, sir?
Guest: I'll have a gin tonic, please.
Waiter: Yes, sir. That's one dry sherry and one gin tonic.
Guest: That's right.

UNIT 4 Exercise 5 [page 29]
Waiter: Are you ready to order now, madam?
Guest: Yes, I am.
What are your specialities today?
Waiter: We have some fresh asparagus from Belgium this week. Are you having a starter, madam?
Guest: Yes. I'd like the asparagus to begin with.
Waiter: What would you like for your main course?
Guest: I'll have the steak, please.
Waiter: How would you like your steak done?
Guest: Well done, please.
What is the main ingredient in Ratatouille?
Waiter: Tomatoes, madam, and some other vegetables.
Guest: Could I have an extra order of Ratatouille with my main course?
Waiter: Yes, of course, madam.
I'll repeat the order: asparagus to start, steak, well done, and an extra order of Ratatouille. Is that right?
Guest: Yes, that's correct.

UNIT 9 Exercise 3 [b] [page 49]

Given below are suggested dialogues for this question. Variations are possible. Check your dialogues with your trainer.

Dialogue 1
Guest: I'd like a table for four, please.
Waitress: I'm very sorry, sir, but the restaurant is full tonight. We have no more tables at the moment.
Guest: But I have a reservation.
Waitress: May I have your name please, sir.

Guest: Collins. C-O-L-L-I-N-S.
Waitress: I'm afraid your name is not in the reservation book. When did you make the reservation, sir?
Guest: Yesterday. I called yesterday and asked for a table at 8 o'clock tonight.
Waitress: I'm sorry about this, sir. We are fully booked now, but if you can wait about an hour, I'll be able to give you a table for four.

Dialogue 2
Guest: This meat is very tough. I can't even cut it!
Waitress: Oh, I'm sorry, sir. The New Zealand rib-eye is usually very tender.
Guest: Then maybe it's over-cooked. I asked for medium to well-done.
Waitress: Yes, that could be the problem. Can I get you another steak or would you like something else for your main course, sir?
Guest: I'll have the steak, but I hope it doesn't take too long.
Waitress: I'll be back as soon as possible. I'm sorry for the inconvenience, sir.

UNIT 11 Exercise 5 [page 57]
Waiter: Would you like any desserts?
Guest [1]: Yes, I'd like the apple tart, please.
Waiter: Certainly, Madam. What about you, sir?
Guest [2]: Just coffee for me.
Waiter: What sort of coffee would you like, sir?
Guest [2]: An espresso, please.
Waiter: Would you like to try our fruit tarts, sir? They are the house specialities.
Guest [2]: No dessert for me, thank you. I've eaten too much.
Waiter: Any coffee for you, madam?
Guest [1]: Yes, I'll have a cappuccino.

UNIT 12 Exercise 5 [page 61]
Could I get you another cup of coffee?
Would you like another cup of coffee?

Could I get you an after-dinner drink?
Would you like an after-dinner drink?

Could I get you some water?
Would you like more water?

Could I get you a liqueur?
Would you like a liqueur?

Could I get you a glass of wine?
Would you like a glass of wine?

Could I get you anything else?
Would you like anything else?

UNIT 13 Exercise 5 [page 65]
Waiter: Here's your card, sir, and your copy of the voucher.
Guest: Thank you.
Waiter: Can I get you anything else?
Guest: No, thank you. We are leaving now.
Waiter: I hope you enjoyed your dinner.
Guest: Yes, we did. It was a very good meal.
Waiter: We hope to see you again soon.
Guest: We'll certainly come again.
Waiter: Thank you very much, sir. Thank you, madam. Goodnight.
Guest: Goodnight.